To my Darling dAughter who helps me to get this book bein published-
Mum

In Spite Of ...
Reflections on Faith

In Spite Of ...
Reflections on Faith

PEARL LENNON

Story Terrace

Text Pearl Lennon

Editor Rebecca Parnaby-Rooke, on behalf of StoryTerrace

Design StoryTerrace

Copyright © Pearl Lennon

First print January 2023

StoryTerrace

www.StoryTerrace.com

FOREWORD

I have recently retired after 40 years of Baptist ministry, the final 16 of which were spent in Forest Gate, East London. Pearl was a member of the church long before I arrived, and we have come to know each other pretty well over the years.

One of the earliest known images of the Christian Church is the ship. Back in the 1st Century, the sea was perceived as a place of danger, with ships tending to hug the shoreline lest catastrophe struck. That turbulent, unpredictable environment seemed a good way of describing the Roman Empire, built as it was on conquest and tyranny. The early Christians had to navigate their way through this Empire faithfully. There were distractions, setbacks, and even persecutions to face. Following Jesus was costly.

These days we see the sea and ships very differently. Few of us aspire to be crew, but many of us would love to be passengers on an ocean cruise. Sadly, that image has begun to infiltrate our churches. Many are content to be Sunday passengers, happy to praise but reluctant to serve. If Jesus had developed the image, I'm pretty sure he would have been using the word 'crew' to describe his followers.

Pearl was always a member of my crew. She was practical,

she was pastoral, and she regularly cooked great dinners for our Friday Lunch Club. She was an avid reader of the scriptures, and she was a leader. As she was turning 80, she thought about writing her autobiography, but then she felt God say to her, '*Rather than write about yourself, why don't you write about me?*' And so, for the next year, as she studied her Bible, Pearl wrote down what she was learning.

Moses, we are told in Deuteronomy 34, lived for 120 years, but according to Acts 7 it was in his 80th year that God appeared to him in a burning bush, and the final 40 years were his most productive. Perhaps Pearl is on a parallel path! Each chapter is short but challenging, focusing on a particular scripture and hopefully unsettling our worlds.

In Victorian London, when churches were packed on Sunday evenings, two friends went to different churches to hear two well-known preachers. When they met again to reflect on what they had heard, one said, 'What a wonderful preacher!' The other responded, 'What a wonderful saviour!'

Pearl will be hoping for the second reaction from you.

Bruce Stokes, retired Minister,
Woodgrange Baptist Church 2021

CONTENTS

OPENING PRAYER

Open our eyes, O Lord. Open our hearts and minds I pray, that as we read your words today, we may be filled with your presence.

Open our ears, O Lord, that we may hear clearly your still, small voice guiding us, teaching us your ways and direction.

Open our lives, O Lord. Show us how to love and embrace both you and others, our dear redeeming Lord. May your words of grace and truth within our soul be stored.

Open our lips, dear Lord, in praise; that we may tell what love imparts the work of grace, about your ways, about your works, within our hearts.

Blow away any hidden agendas and fill us with your holy presence. Unblock the narrowness of our minds and let us feel your presence today, Lord.

You've called us to come near to you, Lord Jesus. So here we are, desiring more of you. Because there's more, Lord, and still more. Please help us to encounter more of you today.

Amen.

The Lord can make our lives like this tree: something that provides shelter to others.

Part One

IN THE BEGINNING

1

A PRAYER OF AWAKENING

My heart is steadfast, O Lord my God. So, I will sing and make music to you. Awake, my soul! Awake! Awake with harp and lyre. I will stand awake at the door, and I will proclaim you Lord among the nations. I will sing and praise your name among the people. So great is your love and your faithfulness, reaching up to the skies and beyond to the heavens, I cannot be silent. Be exalted, O my God, to your place above the heavens; let your glory be over all the Earth.

Holy Father, there is none like you. We want to worship and adore you. We may sometimes fail, yet we know you are merciful, gracious, full of compassion and love. When we fall short you show mercy on us. We are so thankful that you are patient with us.

Thank you for being the compassionate God who still calls us to repentance. Your love for mankind goes beyond bounds, so much so you sent your only son to die for us. Yes, it is true! You do not treat us as we deserve. You continually hold out your hands towards us as a father to a child. Merciful Father, you are so wonderful, so mighty in power and awesome in judgement, I feel so weak and faint in your presence.

Yet I know that you can still use even me in spite of all my faults. I know you did not tell me to leave my Egypt in vain. You have a purpose for my life. Please, Lord, use me here in this street where I live. May my light shine, that others may see you in me. Let the life I live speak for me. I love you, Father, Son and Holy Spirit, and commit my life to you.

Amen.

2

'GLORIFY THE LORD WITH ME; LET US EXALT HIS NAME TOGETHER' (PSALM 34:3)

As I reflected on what it means to 'glorify the Lord', I was reminded of the preceding verse written by the psalmist, 'Let the afflicted hear and rejoice' (Psalm 34:2). I want to take a good look at this, and what it means for us.

To glorify, exalt, hear and rejoice simply means to give to God the highest praise that is due to him. We can do this through talking about him, praising him for all he is, what he has done and all that he is going to do in our lives. We are given examples throughout the Bible on how to do this. These include Nebuchadnezzar, who said he would glorify God after his testimony of what God had done for him (Daniel 4:37), and the psalmist of Psalm 86:12 who also declared he would exalt and glorify the name of the Lord.

David writes, 'Glorify the Lord with me,' and I can tell you, there's nothing sweeter or more pleasant than to continue to talk about the Lord. It's so wonderful. It is a most powerful way of worshipping the Lord. To be in conversation about him is to exalt him. It is especially good if you can even let out a few words about him before the ungodly (see Romans 1:21 and Matthew 5:16).

We are told our good deeds will glorify the Father. So let us talk about him. Let his name just roll off your tongue always, putting him in his rightful place in the presence of the enemy. For we are commissioned to spread the good news of his love to all nations, and what better way to do this than by speaking of his great works in our lives?

Reflection

There are many scriptures which encourage us to lift up the Lord and exalt his name always. For example, 1 Peter 2:12 tells us that God will be glorified on the day he visits us. John 11:4 says to glorify God is to exalt his name in any way. Many of the psalms praise and glorify God, such as the ones already explored in this chapter. As we reflect on these verses, and how they speak into our lives, we ask that God may help us to glorify, exalt and praise him as David did. Amen.

3

'MY BROTHER'S KEEPER'
(GENESIS 4:1-13)

'Comfort, comfort my people', says your God' (Isaiah 40:1). That's what the Lord told his leaders and prophets to do, from Moses to Isaiah to Jesus himself. In Genesis 4, the Israelites, God's chosen people were going through a difficult time and certainly needed some comfort. They were told that they were a 'stiff necked people' as they were rebellious, refusing to honour God and show him the respect that he deserved. So God poured out his wrath upon them, although their punishments never lasted for too long as he loved them so. They were his inheritance, and he would rather they came back to him in repentance and lived, than suffered and died through his discipline.

God is to be respected and worshipped, and those punished through death cannot do either of those things. God wants us to see the error of our ways and come back into his loving care. Even Cain, who killed his brother Abel, was given a mark of protection and allowed to live his life after denying his role as his brother's keeper and committing a deadly sin (Genesis 4:8-15). God is our loving father who paid a great price for our souls, whatever we choose to go on and do with them. So, as in the book of Isaiah, he told his leaders and prophets to comfort the Israelites, offering them a path back to his protection and parenthood; what a wonderful God we have! He was then and still is now.

There's a lot of hurting going on right now. God is still telling his leaders and prophets here and now to comfort his people. The suffering may be different. The people who are suffering may not all be descendants of God's original chosen people (the Jews) or followers of Jesus Christ (Christians), but they are all his creation. He loves us all equally.

John 1:11-13 names those of us who know God directly as the Children of God, but we are still instructed to care for everyone. It's called *agape* love, God's love for human beings. Remember God asked Jonah in chapter four, verse 11, 'And should I not have concern for the great city of Nineveh, in which there are more than a hundred and twenty thousand people who cannot tell their right hand from their left—and also many animals?' Yes, we must! We must show compassion to all beings as our Lord Jesus would.

Hebrews 1:2 tells us God used to speak to us through his prophets, but now he speaks to us through Jesus, his son, and his teachings recorded in the Word. The Holy Spirit quickens our own spirits and enables us to hear from God ourselves. While God's chosen nation was originally the Hebrew people, Jesus died for all of us, Jew or Gentile, and we who choose to hear what the Gospel is saying to us will hear God speaking through his words, no matter who we are. He has poured his spirits into us so we can remain in him, and he in us. We are all brothers in him.

Paul tells us in 2 Corinthians 1:4 that God comforts us in all our troubles so that we may comfort others. We are our brother's keeper, particularly those who are part of the body of Christ but even those who do not worship our Lord Jesus as God's only begotten son. Our brother hurts when we hurt, is sad when we are sad and rejoices with us when we rejoice. We must share in other people's burdens even if they are far away.

When the Delta variant of the COVID-19 virus overwhelmed India I wept with the people there, it was so awful. I am sure Jesus wept too. We must share in their burdens as in their joy, become encouragers and comfort God's people as he told his leaders and prophets to do. Yet, I know this is easier said than done.

When I think of the peak of the COVID-19 pandemic, the point we needed comfort and encouragement the most, we were in lockdown and not allowed to visit anyone. People died alone in hospital with their relatives not able to visit them. How do we comfort family members left behind in such circumstances? I tell you it has not been a good time, as this pandemic left many of us with so much pain, so much sadness and with so many people hurting. We need to find ways to care for each other and be our brother's keepers in this time of great need.

Jesus comforted his disciples when they were hurting, whatever the reasons why. It is not always clear how we can help most of the people who are hurting now, especially those still frightened and worried about being with people, but there are a few things we can do. Keep in touch with those you don't see, make every effort to reach out to those who remain isolated and pray without ceasing. Ask God to send comfort to those we cannot see or hear from. While I know our whole pandemic experience has been really, really sad, we can pray and ask God for peace. The Lord himself will comfort you, and I know this is true for sure. He will come to you if you ask him to, and comfort you as the leaders and prophets have promised.

Reflection

5 Your love, Lord, reaches to the heavens,
   your faithfulness to the skies.
6 Your righteousness is like the highest mountains,
   your justice like the great deep.
   You, Lord, preserve both people and animals.
7 How priceless is your unfailing love, O God!
   People take refuge in the shadow of your wings.
8 They feast on the abundance of your house;
   you give them drink from your river of delights.
9 For with you is the fountain of life;
   in your light we see light.
10 Continue your love to those who know you,
   your righteousness to the upright in heart.

(Psalm 36:5-10)

4

AFTER THE FLOOD
(GENESIS 6:11-9:19)

I cannot think of a time when, as a Church, we have had to wait on God as we have throughout this COVID-19 pandemic. People from every nation all over the world have been brought to their knees. Some countries are better than others at waiting on God, as year after year they go through drought, plague, pestilence or war. Yet this COVID-19 pandemic has forced the whole world to wait on the Lord in this same way. As individual Christians, we have had to develop the virtue of patience. I say develop, as I know God has given us everything we need, but we also have to follow his way to access his gifts. We will not develop them if we do not remain near to God. He has told us, "'3 You who are far away, hear what I have done; you who are near, acknowledge my power!'" (Isaiah 33:13). Therefore, we must listen, stay close and testify to his gifts working out in our lives.

Whether living near to or far from God – and most

were living very far – the people of Genesis must have been horrified when the rain began to fall. You cannot even imagine their experience, bearing in mind it had never rained before. Everything ground to a halt when the rain began, yet no one knew when it was going to stop! Everyone just had to wait on the Lord. In the end, the rain did stop some 40 days later, although the whole Earth and every living thing upon it was drowned. The only life which remained was Noah, his family and two of each animal saved by the ark that God commissioned Noah to build. Through his faithfulness to God and obedience to his instruction, Noah was able to save life on this planet. Isn't that incredible?

Despite the rain stopping after 40 days and 40 nights, Noah and his family had to sit and wait for 150 days for the water to dry up (Genesis 8:3), and yet still longer until the dove brought back an olive branch signifying it was safe to leave the ark (Genesis 8:8-12). This example tells us however long we are waiting on God, whatever it may be for, it will pass. We know that this pandemic is not the end of the world. It may be the beginning of the end, but it's not the end. So, this too will pass. Yet waiting is not really in our make-up. We want to have our every wish met, immediately. We want it yesterday, meaning, as a people, we cannot really wait very well.

I must tell you, waiting for the end of this pandemic has caused me such misery. I felt trapped. I almost went into depression and nearly had a breakdown. My foot almost slipped on my walk with God. I could not see my children, my friends or go to church. We could not celebrate my 80th birthday or my husband's 90th birthday. I was in a bad state.

In the end, one of my children came to see me, and went back to tell the others to come and see me one by one or else they soon would not have a mother! So, they began to visit in spite of the lockdown and that turned things around. God stepped in with his grace and mercy.

I am a homely person by nature. Yet I was angry because someone told me to stay in, and I could not have what I wanted when I wanted it. We are such fickle people. Eventually, I came to my senses and accepted that I had to develop patience. I learned to wait, as Noah did, until it was safe to emerge into the world again.

Prayer

Thank you, Lord, for using this pandemic to show me I need this fruit of the Spirit, patience. I always thought I was a humble person, but I now know I was not. Praise the Lord for this opening of my eyes so I can see myself as God does yet know he has used me anyway. I know I must wait on the Lord, and he will bless me even more, for there is still more to receive. Therefore, I will wait for the Lord as the Watchman waits for the morning. Thank you, Heavenly Father, for your wisdom.

Amen.

5

THE MIGHTY HAND OF GOD (EXODUS 32)

When Moses was a young man, God took him out of Egypt, only to send him back 40 years later. Why would he do this? I believe God wanted Moses to acknowledge what he had done in killing a man (Exodus 2:11-12). He did this accidentally, yes, but God has still given us the commandment, 'Thou shalt not kill' (Exodus 20:13). Moses ran away from Egypt to escape Pharoah's justice, but did not seek to accept God's justice. At the time of his crime, he did not yet know God, but God knew him and had taken note of his action. Moses' heart was known to God and although he had made a mistake, the Lord knew he was a man full of compassion and strength. God knew he could use Moses to show his mighty hand and had great plans to do so.

Before God could give Moses his assignment to lead the Israelites out of Egypt, he had to be sure Moses was ready to acknowledge him (Exodus 3-4). I recognise this situation in my own life. I too did not acknowledge God in my earlier days. I came to know him quite late. But I always knew there was something or someone bigger than myself in life. I have always been a writer, pouring out my troubles onto the page in letters which I would always address to 'Dear God'. I may not have known him, but I knew of him. I am confident he knew me, and his mighty hand was guiding my life towards the day we would meet.

I was born in a Christian household. My mother and father were deacons of the church we used to attend. My father was both a lay preacher and the treasurer, therefore we were a very highly respected family. Three of my sisters and one of my brothers knew the Lord when we were growing up, but I did not have a personal relationship with God as a child. It was not until I was much older, when I had a personal encounter with Jesus, that I gave my heart to God and I have never been the same again! As with Moses and God, I now know the weight of being accountable to someone.

Once your heart has been granted to God, you are responsible for making sure your life reflects his glory and that you are accountable to him only. The story of God's goodness has to be told! Do not believe if you decide to disobey God, you will escape without consequence. When Pharaoh decided to disobey God, by ignoring his call through Moses to let the Israelites go, it was not Pharaoh alone who suffered; the whole country of Egypt suffered for Pharaoh's hard-heartedness (Exodus 7-12). We see this again and again throughout the Bible. Take 1 Chronicles 21:8-13 when King David made an error and all of Israel suffered for it. Even in our family, when one of us falls short the whole family suffers for it. We are given our freedom by God to choose how we live our lives, but if we make poor choices which reflect badly on him we will be held accountable.

It is not often we are called to go back and make amends in life. God was very cross with the Israelites when they craved for the food of Egypt once they had left (Number 11:5). They were meant to be moving forward, not back. None of us gets a free pass out of the mess the world throws us into. We must keep moving on and making the best of it. But Moses did go back as God sent him, leading and guiding him with the support of his siblings Aaron and Miriam to give him strength. He went in the name of the Lord, the great I Am, and through his faithfulness, God has been glorified and renowned forever. It was not without trepidation; Moses was unwilling at first and took some persuasion. But remember, God cannot and should not be challenged, as he is our Lord, and the battle is his.

Prayer

Lord Jesus. As I write this book, I am at the age Moses was when you called him into your service. We thank you for the many great deeds he did in your name, including leading your people out of Egypt and to the promised land through the gift of your mighty power. This epic tale is left on record for us to learn from, and your name has been glorified throughout the world. This was your purpose. You sanctified Israel, set your people aside to be a light to the nations, until the time came for Jesus Christ, Emmanuel, to descend from heaven itself and be revealed as the true light of the world. For this, we can only wonder and thank you, O Lord.

Father, as you have done for your servant Moses, do unto me I pray. I know, O Lord, that nothing is impossible for you, so even at my age, like Caleb, I feel the same now as when you first called me into your service. I pray that you will use this book to inspire great things in those who read it. I pray, Lord, that by your grace, these words will find their way to the people who most need to hear them, that hearts will be softened and minds will be turned towards you.

Thank you, great Father, for your grace and mercy. Thank you for our Lord Jesus Christ, our Saviour, and thank you for allowing us to show the world who you are through the tasks you give us to do for you.

Amen.

6

THE AWESOME GOD
(JEREMIAH 29:11)

Aren't we blessed to have an awesome God who has a plan and purpose for each of us? Let us look for a moment at the tale of the man who was born blind (John 9). The question is asked 'Rabbi, who sinned, this man or his parents, that he was born blind?' (John 9:2). The Lord explained there was no sin, but 'this happened so that the works of God might be displayed in him.' (John 9:4). Therefore, when a child is born different, should we question why as the apostles did? Do we ever think God could be glorified through that child? I believe that is so.

I used to be a carer and have seen many things in my time working with people who experience the world differently from me. I have seen a depth of love I did not know existed through spending time with them. That is not to say it is not difficult at times, with many challenges to meet. But I can safely say, yes, God can be glorified through people with all types of disabilities and difficulties. I believe God is using many, if not all of them, to fulfil his plans.

We know that God had a plan for the man born blind as he does for all of us. A plan to prosper, not to harm (Jeremiah 29:11). But the timing for God is so wonderful! To think God knew this man was going to be healed, but he waited for the opportune time to do it, when Jesus would be there. He watched over the man, guiding him through his struggle in life without sight and keeping him safe from harm. It pleased God to keep him waiting until his time was ready and his purpose could be fulfilled. God's name was to be glorified before the unbelievers through his glorious son, Jesus Christ. Yet it was not all good news.

The time God chose for Jesus to meet the blind man and heal him was on the Sabbath day, the day of rest. Jesus healed him anyway, even though he knew doing so would stir up his enemies. That mattered not. God's will must be done come what may. In this same way, God put Pharaoh in a specific position so his purposes would be revealed, hardening his heart so that he wouldn't let the Israelites go even if he may have previously been inclined to. (Exodus 9:16). God's name must be renowned throughout the world, and the world must see his power.

God's plan for the world is still moving forward even today. He is working out his purposes even now. If you think of how far you have come since you were called by God, you will see what I mean. However, there is always more to come. For instance, the mother and father of that man born blind must have given up on him ever having sight again, thinking that if he was born blind, he could not be healed. But God showed them that he was still working out his plan through his son healing theirs.

God knew the blind man before he was even born. So, it is with all of us. Think about this. Jesus Christ was at the creation, yet it took him thousands of years to reveal himself to us. Since all of us are works in progress and God does not do anything in vain, he has a plan for each and every one of us to prosper when our time comes. It might not be as drastic in revelation as the ministry of Jesus, or in the outcome as the healing of this man born blind, but God's name is to be glorified and he will do whatever it takes – and we have a part to play in that! 'There are different kinds of working, but in all of them and in everyone it is the same God at work.' (1 Corinthians 12:6). So let us leave the space and time in our lives for God, so that he may have his own way with us, to reveal his awesomeness and bestow the blessings upon us which lie in store.

Prayer

Loving Heavenly Father, as I looked back on the story of this man born blind and saw how you've worked out your plans and purposes to bring glory to your name, it reminded me that you have a plan for me too, even at this age. So, with all my heart, soul and mind I surrender to you my all in all and offer up my life to you, even now with those precious words, 'Here I am, take me'. Thank you, Heavenly Father, for allowing me to have a glimpse of you. It is most honourable, and I will praise you always.

Amen.

7

JACOB WRESTLES WITH
THE ANGEL (GENESIS 31:38-51)

Moving on in life is not easy, as Jacob found out when he had to spend all night wrestling with the Angel to be allowed past (Genesis 32:24). Jacob told Laban, his mother and brother that his escape from Paddan Aram with his wives, children and livestock was because the Lord had seen how hard he had laboured over the past 21 years. I do not think this is the case. It is not the labour of our hands which fulfils the Lord's requirements for restoration. Jacob's own prayer (Genesis 32:9-12) shows his recognition of his unworthiness in God's eyes. Yet he did not repent of the wrongs he had done to his brother Esau, showing only fear at meeting him again. So, twenty years after robbing Esau, in collusion with their mother, Jacob is now coming back home under God's guidance but with unfinished business.

It is clear God has a plan for Jacob and God's will must be done. Restoration must be achieved, hence the wrestling match. God was changing Jacob through the bout. The wrestling match drained Jacob physically, and his hip was put out of joint. He walked with a limp following that fight. God totally reformed his spirit, changing his name from Jacob to Israel in recognition of the transformation in him. His pride was broken, and he became humble. He was now the man God could use to fulfil his promise and purposes. God's plan would now succeed, but Jacob needed to transform from the scheming man of his youth to become one of the giants of the Bible.

Great men who have done great things for God have to change their ways and humble themselves before God to be useful to him, and we are no different. Moses spent his time in the wilderness. Isaiah, the great prophet, did not really get deep into God's works until King Uzziah died, then he was called to do great things for God (Isaiah 6). David went through tragedy and war before he became king. When Simon Peter got reinstated, only then did the real work begin (John 21:5-19). In spite of what we do, or how we behave, God will do what he has to do to fulfil his purposes. Even if that means wrestling with us for a night.

Reflection

God has not changed, will not change nor can we do anything to change God's mind about us. Yes, we may delay his plans with our actions at times, but they will be done. May God help us to take these things into consideration. As we read our Bible, may we gain further understanding, trusting God to fulfil his promises in our life. May we pray 'Let your kingdom come, may your will be done in us through Jesus Christ. Amen.' – and truly mean it.

8

LIVING BY GOD'S LEADING
(EXODUS 16-17)

Where are we in our lives right now? Are we wandering the wilderness searching for Canaan? Or have we reached the Promised Land? By Exodus 16, it is over 30 years since the Israelites left Egypt, yet they have not reached Canaan. It has been a long, arduous journey for them, as it is for us today. The children of Israel did not have the Holy Bible to follow, but they did have a pillar of cloud by day and a pillar of fire by night (Exodus 13:21-22). As our ancestors needed God's assistance to guide them, so do we. He travels with us on life's journey even through our own wilderness experiences. (see Chapter 12). He gave us the words of the psalmist in Psalm 119:105, '105 Your word is a lamp to my feet and a light to my path', directing us back to the Bible for our guidance in today's time of need.

If we let God lead, he will be there for us, guiding and protecting us from our enemies. He looks after his own. We can access his words of guidance through the Bible, all in our own homes! Isaiah the prophet says God spoke to him when he wrote (Isaiah 50:4) and God still speaks to us even now. He also gave us the Holy Spirit, named 'The Comforter' by our Lord Jesus himself (John 16:7). We do not see him, but if we believe what Jesus told us about himself, and desire him to be closer to him personally, we can have him residing with us as the children of Israel had God residing with them in those columns of fire and smoke.

Jesus remains with us always if we choose to let him into our hearts. He promises he will never leave us. In Deuteronomy 4:29 we are assured '29 But if from there you seek the Lord your God, you will find him if you seek him with all your heart and with all your soul.' and in John 15:5 Jesus tells his disciples 'If you remain in me and I in you, you will bear much fruit'. Isaiah tells us in chapter 45, verse 19, God did not ask the Israelites to leave Egypt in vain, nor does he ask us to bear our burdens without cause. God loves us with unfathomable love. He has a plan for all of us and it is just glorious when God's plans come to fruition. The only condition is we must not lean on our own understanding, only on him.

The Israelites dutifully followed their columns of fire and cloud through the desert on their way to cross the desert from the Red Sea to the Promised Land, a journey that should take 11 days. Instead, it took them more than a lifetime, through their disobedience and insistence on leaning on their own understanding. Because of this, the original exiles missed out on the wonderful things God held in store for them. His promise and plans were withheld, to be bestowed on future generations instead.

So, what is the real lesson in all of this? It is wise to stay under the leadership of our God and saviour of the universe, who will then fulfil his words and promises in our life.

Reflection

Is Jesus truly the king of your heart today? Are you obedient to God in everything that you do? Do you read and take direction from your Bible every day? Live by God's leading and all will be well. Lean on your own understanding and who knows what blessings you could be missing out on?

9

WE SHALL SEE HIM FACE TO FACE (EXODUS 32)

If we could grasp that we will see God face to face someday, it would surely revolutionise our way of thinking. But should we need to see God face to face for our attitudes to change? Are we seeing him now, or are we working to see him? If we are not seeing him, why not? Could we see him now if we changed our ways? If we are not seeing God face to face every day, then we might as well be like those who do not know God at all. We, who are near him, should be enjoying being in his presence daily. And if we say that's not seeing him, then we would be like the Israelites who made the golden calf because they wanted to see their God when they had the columns of fire and smoke leading them every day. They were not contented with the knowledge of him watching over them, giving them manna every day. They created an idol to suit their own needs, instead of trusting in God for them.

It is not uncommon for people to want to see God face

to face. Indeed, all through the Old Testament, we are encouraged to seek God's face. Moses asked God several times to let him see his face, and David, a man after God's heart, insisted that we must seek God's face in many of his psalms (e.g. Psalm 46, 27, 8, 105). But no one can see God's face and live, not until we get to heaven. I think the Old Testament writers meant we should seek to be in God's presence and see his glory, so we can reflect it back into the world. We need only to look around us in our daily walk with our saviour, Jesus Christ, to see his glory since the world is filled with it. That should be sufficient for us while we are here on Earth. This makes me think that it was the presence of God which was being carried around by the Israelites in the Ark of the Covenant. They did not have much faith if they were still seeking God's presence when he was housed amongst them!

This brings me back to the golden calf. When it came to their God, the Israelites weren't satisfied with a presence, they wanted something to see. This still happens today as people across the world have found something to worship other than God, their creator. Some countries have lots of Gods, and in some countries, people worship their leaders instead. The world is full of distracting things that can keep us from seeking God's face more earnestly, such as our mobile telephones and fancy computers; some might say we have turned to worship those now too. They become obstacles. Idols. Our own golden calves.

Jesus knew there would always be people who want to see God. So, he puts it plainly in the Beatitudes. 'Blessed are the pure in heart, for they shall see God' (Matthew 5:8). The author of Hebrews warns 'Make every effort to live in peace with everyone and to be holy; without holiness no one will see the Lord.' (Hebrews 12:4), and Revelation 22:4 assures us when we get to heaven, we shall see his face. See how none of these words of encouragement tells us we have to be intelligent, wise, or well learned in order to see God? No, we are encouraged to live lives of holiness to please God. We may study, not to be wiser than anyone else, but to be knowledgeable about our scriptures. For it is through their guidance we will live well and stay on the path to seeing God, face to face, in heaven.

It is important to note that Jesus focuses on our hearts, the most difficult part of us to keep pure. If everything is right with your heart, everything will be right with God. Yet it is almost impossible to keep a pure heart. I say almost, as all things are indeed possible through Christ Jesus. If it was not for his grace, it would be impossible, because the heart is so deceitful. It is the seat of trouble. But thanks be to God, through Christ Jesus, grace is available. Our sinful nature can and does try to change our attitude, make excuses and put the blame on others, e.g. the church, the preaching or teaching, but with a renewal of our thinking by the power of the Holy Spirit, it is possible to keep our hearts pure and therefore see God's face.

Look again at Exodus 32. The Israelites made that idol of gold because they wanted to see something. Let us not be so foolish. As Jesus told Thomas in the upper room following his resurrection, blessed are those whose faith is so strong they believe without having to see something first (John 20:29). We don't need to see God yet. We are a people of faith, not sight. Therefore, let us enjoy God's presence through faith alone on our walk with him here on Earth. While it is indeed sweet and powerful to desire him so much, and sometimes we long for him so, there will be plenty of time to gaze upon God's face in heaven. Let us draw close to him now.

Reflection

Turn your eyes upon Jesus
Look full, in his wonderful face
And the things of Earth will grow strangely dim
In the light of his glory and grace

('Turn Your Eyes Upon Jesus'
by Helen H. Lemmel)

10

MAKE TIME TO BE HOLY
(JOSHUA 1:8)

God's desire for us is that we all should be holy. That's what he calls us to be, holy as he is holy (Leviticus 11:44). This is why we are directed to make special sacrifices and prayer offerings, to honour God. It is not about the labour of our hands but about lavishing that portion of offering to God, making that sacrifice of toil and time with a pure heart. This is what pleases the Lord. Good intention is important, and you should be seen to act righteously, not in the extravagant way of the Pharisees, but in a humble way. Isaiah 43:22-24 tells us when we are not doing these things God still bears the burden of our sin, which angers him. So, we must make time for him.

The Lord Jesus has given us the Beatitudes to guide us in practical ways to make time for God (Matthew 5:1-12). Read them, put them into practice and embody the spirituality. Try to follow Jesus' instructions; ask yourself daily, 'What would Jesus do?' Take the words of God to your heart and do not ever put them away, for as we learned in Chapter 3, God's words never change and are meant to last forever. Stand on what you've learned from your parents and your priest if you believe their teaching is right. Stand on the words of God and the promises he has made to us. Those who believe don't follow any new teaching; there is no new teaching as God's Word is unchanging. As it was in the beginning, so it shall be in the end.

Reflection

'Keep this Book of the Law always on your lips; meditate on it day and night, so that you may be careful to do everything written in it. Then you will be prosperous and successful.' (Joshua 1:8).

As God told Joshua to read his holy text, so he tells us we should read our Bibles. The words are God's words and will sustain us through all things.

11

JESUS IS STILL CALLING

When we accepted the Lord in our life, somehow or other we heard him say, 'Come to me, all you who are weary and burdened, and I will give you rest' (Matthew 11:28). We said yes to his call, and the rest is history.

How thankful we are, and how wonderful God is for causing us to hear this calling. I think he was calling to me for some time before I accepted it and acknowledged his calling. I know he forgave my ignorance, and I do not think he only calls us once. We are told he called Samuel three times (1 Samuel 3:8-9). The Bible says Samuel did not recognise God's voice because he did not know his voice yet. I think this is often true for most of us. We do not always understand what is happening when we hear God calling us to repentance, but thankfully God does not give up on us in our uninformed state and keeps calling to us.

Often, there will be some sort of trigger, an event in our lives or something changing within us that alerts us of God's calling. Suddenly things we used to do in our lives which would not be pleasing to him, we do not want to do anymore. It is suggested Timothy's mother and grandparents could have been praying for Paul, laying the foundations for his conversion (2 Timothy 1:5). Likewise, I think my mother and father were praying for me for a long time before I said yes to Jesus. Nonetheless, whichever way I came to the Lord, I am inexpressibly glad and thankful that I did. I know I have missed out on the knowledge of his parenthood for many years in my youth, but since I accepted him, I have been catching up on all the good things he has to offer me.

It is never too late to say yes to Jesus. He is still calling us to come to him. When the world seems to be falling in on us, God is still reaching out his hands telling us to call him Father. We can bring all our cares, troubles, doubts, fears and anxieties to him, and he will care for us as one does for their beloved children. Look at the way he blessed Ephraim through Israel in spite of his birth order (Genesis 48:19). God's love is unbounding, especially if you are trying to walk in his light.

Through God's amazing love, we can be secure in the knowledge we have someone to turn to, whenever we feel sad, lonely or despairing. He draws near to us when we are tired and says, 'Come away with me. Let's go and have some rest.' Though we may think he only calls us once to save us from the world of sin, I am here to tell you there is that and more, for he is calling us still to come to him however long we have walked with him. He still asks us to come and spend time with him. Isn't that wonderful? Isn't he marvellous? He tells us to bring our pain, sadness, disappointment, doubt and fear to him, lay our burdens down, and we will find rest for our weary souls.

We are God's beloved children and the sheep of the shepherd. In telling us how much God cares for us, Psalm 18:16-17 says, 'He reached down from on high and took hold of me; he drew me out of deep waters. He rescued me from my powerful enemy, from my foes, who were too strong for me.'

So, we come to God every day not only to be saved from our sin or to repent of our guilty consciences but also to bow down and worship him, knowing he has rescued us, protects us still and keeps us from powers greater than we can bear. Thank you, O Lord.

So, I advise you to gather together, in your small groups or congregations of many, and worship the Lord by talking about him and bringing all your troubles to him. 2 Corinthians 1:3 reminds us he is the God of all comfort, so I encourage you to get to know his voice if you do not already. We are his sheep. We ought to know our shepherd's voice. I ask you now to picture our Lord Jesus coming to our help when things seem to get the better of us. I can imagine seeing him stretching out his arm towards me saying 'Come'. Let me tell you, when I imagine this, I run into his arms. Whether you fall on your knees, or however you respond, just humble yourself before him and he will take care of you.

Prayer

Our loving Heavenly Father, how I thank you for your omnipresence, O loving God. You are so wonderful to us. We were so unworthy of your loving kindness, grace and mercy, yet you still call us to come and be taken care of. Thank you for accepting us just as we are, Lord. We have accepted your invitation and come to you weary, wounded and scared, knowing your healing and comfort await us.

Praise and thanks to you, Father. Thank you for your unconditional love.

Amen.

12

A WILDERNESS EXPERIENCE
(1 SAMUEL 22:1-2)

A wilderness experience for us is likely to be very different from the one our Lord Jesus had (Matthew 4:1-11). The fact he was led into the wilderness by the Holy Spirit to face temptation tells me our wilderness experience is likely to be different. Few of us have 90 days to spend in the desert finding ourselves! I also think of Moses' journey, in his youth and then with the Israelites following their flight from Egypt (Exodus). I think those wilderness experiences were God's doing too, that Moses was being disciplined by God so he could be used for greater purposes (see Chapter 5). Being in the wilderness can be for many different reasons and come in many different forms.

I think we are in the midst of a wilderness experience right now. I write this chapter in March 2021 when the world is going through a very dark time with the COVID-19 pandemic. Everywhere is locked down, the streets have no people on them, no stores are open. Even the church doors are locked. The only places open are takeaway restaurants and pharmacies. So many, many people have already died from this virus, with worse to come. If this is a wilderness experience, I know it will only get worse before it gets better.

Those of us who are believers draw closer to our God during times of wilderness experiences. David grew closer to God during his time living in the wilderness (1 Samuel 20-30) and expected great things from him, as recorded in his many psalms composed at the time. Indeed, these wilderness experiences can be turned to for God's purposes.

I am writing this book during this time of COVID-19. I have tried three times before to write and have not succeeded until now. God's timing is perfect. Our Lord Jesus' time in the wilderness was for his good before he began his ministry, therefore we should look for the good in our own wilderness experiences.

David was a strong man mentally, physically and spiritually, but he was still going through a very difficult time with his King, Saul, whose service he was in and whom he had loved. Once Saul became jealous of David's blessings and turned on him, David escaped and went into the wilderness to hide. As it happened, there were many other peoples who were discontented with life and the way things were turning out for them under Saul's rule. They too were having a wilderness experience. Once they heard David had come to the caves in the wilderness, they sought him out. The Bible records their number as 400 which was enough to form an army (1 Samuel 22:1-2). Note that David did not go looking for reinforcements. This was God's intervention in David's life. May God protect us so, in our hour of need.

Just as David found refuge living in a cave in Addulum with God, we can find our refuge in Christ Jesus. He is our rock of the ages. We can always ask him to let us hide ourselves in him. He is always willing and waiting to hold us in his arms and comfort us in times of trouble. Whatever season we are in, God will be our cave if we let him. Job asks, 'Shall we accept good from God, and not trouble?' (Job 2:10). We are God's children; we need discipline which is not always pleasant. May we consider more of his mercy shown to us in grace and not on our own understanding. But remember, when we walk with the Lord, even the wilderness light can shine on us there and we will find ourselves in his glory.

Prayer

Lord Jesus, I thank you for being who you are to us. We praise you for being always in our lives. We thank you for being our hiding place so that we know we can always run into your arms. We thank you for being our prophet and priest. We are so grateful that all we are as your children is to be found in you. We ask you today, help us please to always seek you out, in the knowledge we will always find you.

Thank you for being everything for us. Thank you, Lord.

Amen.

13

MAKING GOOD DECISIONS IN THE MIDST OF A STORM

I t is never easy to make good decisions about the path ahead when we are in the middle of a storm. It takes a strong person to be decisive in their choices when things are at their worst. For example, David chose wisely while he was in one of the biggest storms of his life, with Saul trying to kill him by chasing him over hills and valleys. David could have killed Saul instead to ensure his own safety, yet he decided not to touch God's anointed king (1 Samuel 24).

Bad things done in good times are often remembered and talked about, like the tale of David and Bathsheba (2 Samuel 11). But we seldom talk about the good things done out of our strength in God when things are not going well, such as David sparing Saul.

Paul made a good decision when he was on a ship to Rome, judging the light winds as the precursor to a major storm and warning the captain accordingly (Acts 27:9-44). Unfortunately, since he was a prisoner being transported at that time, he was ignored. So, the crew had to go through a very rough patch before finding safety again. Yet one thing we know as believers in Christ Jesus, if we ask him to come into our boat with us, is that we can smile at the storm and always be safe (Mark 4:35-41). We have got a lot of biblical advice to listen to and follow if we choose to obey.

The Bible is our roadmap on our Christian journey. In the Book of Proverbs, Solomon reminds us not to lean on our own understanding but put our trust in the Lord (Proverbs 3:5-6). In the Old Testament, kings and prophets talked to God all the time and they listened to him. Those who did not (or would not) listen to God, believing in their own power and strength, always ended up suffering for their disobedience. Yet those who stayed close to God were blessed by him.

Hezekiah, one of Israel's kings known for staying close to God, made the good decision to call on God when he was in the midst of his storm, a terminal illness. He turned to God as we all should and told a story of what God had done for him (2 Kings 20:2-3). Yes, we all make mistakes, some bad ones too. But our gracious God is merciful and compassionate. He will cover us through them all, and in Hezekiah's case gave him fifteen extra years of life to live.

Saul did not handle his storm very well. When his storm came, he blamed someone else. That is the way we sometimes avoid facing up to things; it is never you. It is someone else. Saul tried to kill David, but God was in David's boat, praise the Lord! Saul had made a bad decision.

Jezebel made a bad decision when she threatened God's servant Elijah with murder (1 Kings 19:1-2). She paid for it with her life (2 Kings 9:30-33). Samson made a bad decision to disobey God when he married someone that was not a Jewish descendant (Judges 14-15). He ended up under Delilah's thumb (Judges 16:4-31). Abram too made a very bad decision when he went to bed with Hagar, his wife's servant (Genesis 16). We have to face up to the consequences of our decisions when we do not involve God in them.

It is never a bad thing to have Christ Jesus in our boat. One may say if you are a servant of Christ Jesus, it is difficult not to have him with you at all times. We thank God it is not us holding his hands, but him holding ours. He loves us to bits, whatever decisions we make.

Prayer

Holy Father, I thank you for your words given to us through the Bible. We are grateful to have all the tools in that book to use in the time of our storm. Besides, we know you will always be there with us. Thank you for being ours, always. Please help us to remember your words and use them accordingly. To be strong and courageous as you assure us you will always be there for us. Thank you, Father for these examples that have been left on record to help us on our journey. Praise be unto you, O God.

Amen.

14

GIVING GOD OUR BEST
(1 KINGS 6:19-30)

God deserves the best of everything. That's why he insisted that the first fruit of your field should be his (Leviticus 23:10), the first son from your womb (Exodus 13:2), the 1st hour of your day (Psalm 90:14) and even the first-born animal from your flock (Deuteronomy 15:19-21). Starting your day with an hour of prayer is not always possible, especially if your day starts at 4 am(!), however, some people do manage it. In the hustle and bustle of life, it gets harder and harder for us to make time for prayer. Yet God demands such things, and he ought to get the best for he is worthy of it.

I want to talk about giving God the best. That does not always mean time or things. It can mean doing a task, for example, even if it is hard. We should try our best always, do the best we can, give him the best of us and hold him in the highest esteem. Sometimes gifts are not accepted, yet this is due to the manner in which they were offered. For example, in Genesis 4:3-7, Cain offered up his gift from his field, but God did not accept it. I do not think it was the best Cain could do and that is why his gift was rejected.

There is a king in the Bible who at one point in his life did offer God the very best. This was Solomon. He built a vast temple for God designed by his father, David. However, God told David that Solomon should be the one to construct the monument. Why? You may ask. David was a soldier. He had killed a lot of people in his time, so his hands were bloody. This temple was going to be the house of God. It had to be pure and holy.

Just imagine walking into that temple when it was finished. Donald Trump's Mar-a-Lago Resort in Florida would have to close its doors. Having read this Bible passage over and over, I still cannot imagine how richly it was decorated. At first, I did not see the reason why Solomon did it like that, either. I thought to myself, why all this gold? Was it really necessary? It was not until I realised this was Solomon giving his best, doing it all for the Lord Almighty, that it made sense. If this temple was being built to be God's house, it had to be the best, for nothing is too good for him. Not only that, but all the gold and cedar trees belonged to God anyway; why should they not be used in such a way for his glory?

Solomon learned from his father David that we should not give God anything less than full value, and we should treat all that comes from God as fully valuable also (1

Chronicles 21:24). Heeding this lesson wisely, Solomon was generous beyond words, to others and towards God. He knew the value of his wealth, and the expectation he should do much with it, as our Lord Jesus emphasised in one of his parables (Luke 12:47-48). In truth, we all receive a great amount from God, so we ought to thank God with all our heart and be very generous towards him, remembering that all of us have received everything we have from him.

Reflection

Were the whole realm of nature mine,
That were a present far too small;
Love so amazing, so divine,
Demands my soul, my life, my all.

('When I Survey the Wondrous Cross'
by Isaac Watts)

15

HEZEKIAH TELLS HIS STORY (2 KINGS 18-20, 2 CHRONICLES 29-32 & ISAIAH 38-40)

The songwriter Timothy Dudley-Smith wrote in his famous hymn:

Tell out, my soul, the greatness of the Lord!
Unnumbered blessings give my spirit voice;
Tender to me the promise of His Word;
In God my Saviour shall my heart rejoice.
            ('Tell Out, My Soul' by Timothy Dudley-Smith)

That was Mary, Mother of Jesus' song as well (Luke 1:46-55). After she was given the news about her pregnancy by the Angel Gabriel, she did tell out everything her soul had to share, to her cousin Elizabeth. The Samaritan woman from John 4 told out everything her soul had to share with her village as the first evangelist. In fact, there are lots of people written about in the Bible who told out their stories and gave great testimonies. I am certain that all of us can give testimony to the greatness of the Lord. That is also what Hezekiah did.

At a young age, Hezekiah had fallen ill and was about to die. However, he was a God-fearing King, and God remembered that. God sent the prophet Isaiah to tell Hezekiah to put his house in order, at which he became very distressed and started crying out to God, reminding God of how he walked wholeheartedly before him and always did what was right and good in his sight. 2 Kings 20:5-6 tells us God instructed Isaiah to 'Go back and tell Hezekiah, the ruler of my people, "This is what the Lord, the God of your father David, says: I have heard your prayer and seen your tears; I will heal you. On the third day from now you will go up to the temple of the Lord. I will add fifteen years to your life. And I will deliver you and this city from the hand of the king of Assyria. I will defend this city for my sake and for the sake of my servant David."' God called Hezekiah 'the ruler of my people' as a mark of honour, and agreed to extend his life.

Despite the confidence God showed in him, Hezekiah asked Isaiah for a sign. Could it be he still doubted God? Well, after all we are just flesh and blood. Anyhow, God indulged him, and in verse 11 we see God caused the sun's shadow, which had fallen on the stairway of Ahaz, to go back ten steps as the sign that he would do what he had promised. I think God wanted this miracle to be noticed and remembered by all who knew about Hezekiah's illness. Remember, this is the awesome God who lavishes love on the children of men, Adam's fallen race. Hezekiah had to tell the world what God can do, thus glorifying his name and making his grace known.

There is nothing at all in life more worth telling, or talking about, than the receiving of grace and salvation in our lives. There is nothing in all the world so wonderful, so amazing and so good. Following our experiences of salvation through grace from God, we all have a great story to be told. I give thanks and praise to God that some of these testimonies are recorded in the Bible so we can read them and be inspired by them now, such as the testimony of Hezekiah.

Hezekiah's story reminds us that there is not anything too hard for God. What God has shown he can do in one person's life, he can do to anyone he chooses. This is the same God who had done so many astonishing things before Hezekiah's healing. This God opened the sea to let about one million people pass through on dry land. This God held the stars in his hand and threw them into space, causing them to stay in place with nothing to hold them. Is there anything too hard for him?

Look at what he says he'll do for all of us if we return to him and acknowledge him as our God and ruler of the Universe: "'Bring the whole tithe into the storehouse, that there may be food in my house. Test me in this,' says the Lord Almighty, "and see if I will not throw open the floodgates of heaven and pour out so much blessing that there will not be room enough to store it."' (Malachi 3:10). God said he would throw open the windows of heaven for us. Has he done that yet for you in your life?

I am sure you have a story and a testimony, maybe even big ones. They need to be told, as in so doing we are giving God the glory which belongs to him. There are many more people in the bible who shared testimony of God's awesome works done in their lives. I think of Hannah, who conceived Samuel after laying herself before God (Samuel 1). Blind Bartimaeus got his healing (Mark 10:46-52). The woman who was bent over for 18 years got her desire (Luke 13:10-17), and so can we. May we be bold enough to tell our stories. as these people did, thus giving God the praise he truly deserves.

Prayer

Lord Jesus, we thank you for recording the experiences of others, those that had a story to tell. Thank you for the many wonderful stories and testimonies of your great and awesome deeds that worked in the lives of your people, such as King Hezekiah. Thank You, O Lord, that you instructed some of them to write their stories down, to help us on our walk with you. Praise and thanks to you almighty God.

I pray, O Lord, that as I write these words, you may bless them and allow them to be of some encouragement to others. Thank you, Heavenly Father.

Amen.

16

OPPORTUNITIES AND OPPOSITION (NEHEMIAH 1-6)

Opportunity will come our way in life, but where there is opportunity there is often also opposition. That is why the story of Nehemiah is so useful to us Christians, as part of the Word of God. Even though the devil devises schemes to put obstacles in our way, I believe that God wants us to acknowledge our opportunity in the face of such opposition, especially when we are doing his good works. If we want to succeed in life, we will meet opposition. It is how we deal with it that matters. Let us take Nehemiah's example into consideration.

Nehemiah was a cup bearer in the court of the Persian King, one of many Judeans descended from those exiled in Babylon after the fall of Jerusalem. Nehemiah 1:1-4 tells us:

In the month of Kislev in the twentieth year, while I was in the citadel of Susa, Hanani, one of my brothers, came from Judah with some other men, and I questioned them about the

Jewish remnant that had survived the exile, and also about Jerusalem.

They said to me, 'Those who survived the exile and are back in the province are in great trouble and disgrace. The wall of Jerusalem is broken down, and its gates have been burned with fire.'

When I heard these things, I sat down and wept. For some days I mourned and fasted and prayed before the God of heaven.

Nehemiah wept for his brethren living in and around Jerusalem, and also for the city itself. He may have been an exile in a foreign land, yet when he heard that the city wall was on fire, his heart was broken. It lay heavily on his mind, and so it should to all of us. If the house of God is being damaged or used in a disrespectful way, we should be angry! It is the house of God. It should be respected! So, Nehemiah decided to go back to Jerusalem and rebuild the walls.

Firstly, Nehemiah had to ask permission from the King to leave court, and he also asked permission from God in prayer. He was a Jew, one blessed by God. His enemies were Gentiles. They did not believe in God, so they set about to oppose him. Chapter 2:19-20 tells us, 'But when Sanballat the Horonite, Tobiah the Ammonite official and Geshem the Arab heard about it, they mocked and ridiculed us. What is this you are doing? they asked. "Are you rebelling against the king?" I answered them by saying, "The God of heaven will give us success. We his servants will start rebuilding, but as for you, you have no share in Jerusalem or any claim or historic right to it."'

Whenever God gives us something to do, or lays something on our minds, the devil will surely try to stop us with ridicule, shame, mocking or accusations of rebelliousness. We have to rise above it and trust, as Nehemiah did, that the God of heaven will give us success. In Nehemiah's case, he went on to build the walls of Jerusalem bigger and better than ever before.

These sort of obstacles the devil placed in Nehemiah's path can easily be put in front of us. Simple little things can put us off doing things we want to do. If we lean into what we know of God and his words to us, if we rely on them with confidence, we can overcome them. In Genesis 15:11, Abram was making an offering to God and birds of prey came down to spoil his sacrifice, but he drove them away. That was a direct attempt from the devil to oppose his godly deed, but he did not succeed against Abram, nor against Nehemiah, nor against us if we stand firm on what we know of God our Father. God help us against the Sanballats of this day.

Reflection

Nehemiah 4:1-End

Nehemiah did not just sit there waiting on God when his enemies continued to hound him, even bringing their friends along to cause trouble. No, he did something. He continued to build, set guards and God was with him. We need to remember Nehemiah's God is our God too and he is not partial. He will help us as he helped those before us.

17

GOD USES HIS PEOPLE ON EARTH

God can use anyone or anything he chooses. He used Amos, a simple farmer, to prophesise to the nations (Amos 1-9). He used a servant girl to get the attention of Naaman, the commander of the King of Aram's army, in order to reveal his healing power (2 Kings 5). He used Gideon who thought of himself as nothing, born as he was from the smallest tribe of Israel. The Midianites were sending raiding parties who continued to provoke the Israelites by destroying their crops. God was watching over them and responded as the nation cried out for help by calling Gideon to their aid (Judges 6-7). He heeded their prayers.

When the going gets tough there is nothing better than taking your problems to God in prayer. King Jehoshaphat went to the Lord in prayer when facing a whole army and in despair about what to do. God reassured him and saved his people (2 Chronicles 20). Solomon thought he was too young to rule as King over the Israelites. Through talking regularly to God in prayer he was greatly used by God and well regarded across the land. Jeremiah also thought he was too young to be a prophet. He said to God when he was called as a prophet, "'Alas, Sovereign Lord," I said, "I do not know how to speak; I am too young.'" (Jeremiah 1:6). Yes, God can and does use anyone or anything to fulfil his purposes.

If we look at all the different people God has used and in so many different ways, we can truly believe we are all his hands and feet on earth, ready for when he wants to use us to bring his glorious works to pass on Earth. Did he not use a girl no more than thirteen years old in Mary to bring his son to this Earth? All through the Old Testament, God uses people and things to do his bidding, right into the New Testament when our Lord Jesus appears.

Prayer

May God help us to remember who we are before him and before humankind and know that even in our old age God can still use us. God promises to renew our strength if we only make ourselves available to him, and his words stand forever. As God used Gideon, Solomon and Jeremiah, Amos, Mary and Jehosaphat, so may we too be used.

Amen.

18

THE PATIENCE OF JOB

Patience is one of the fruits of the Spirit, and I think it is probably the hardest one to grow. A tough fruit, possibly a dry coconut or a hard nut. I also think you have not truly come up against the need for patience until you suffer for a long time or see the sufferings of people you care about in your own life. At first, I was not sure if angels would experience patience since they are not able to suffer, but then I considered they have been known to wait on us in our distress and suffering. For example, in Judges 13:9-17 when Samson's Mother and Father cause an angel to complain of being detained and in 1 Chronicles 21 when the destroyer angel waited on God and David to decide the fate of Jerusalem.

However, it is a different kind of patience to this which Paul writes about in Galatians 5:22 as the fruit of the Spirit, which the NIV version of the Bible translates as 'forbearance'. This kind of patience will have to be tried and tested. We will only know we have it if we go through tough times. We have all heard about the patience of Job. Job did not learn to develop patience among his herd of camels, his large flock of sheep or his ten children! No, it was through his suffering as he went from one disaster to another.

First Job had to face the death of all ten children in one day. The wiping out of his cattle came in another day and the personal, physical destruction of his body followed the next. All came suddenly with no warning or reason, yet he held on to his faith. That is patience. It was like the whole world just caved in on him all of a sudden, but he held on to his faith. May God help us to be strong as Job!

I believe patience such as Job's is to be found in the depths of the sea of affection, and it is there to be nurtured. God has given all of it to all of us, who receive Him as our Lord and our God. Christ Jesus has given us all of himself, and with this comes his forbearance. Romans 5:3-5 says, 'we also glory in our sufferings, because we know that suffering produces perseverance; perseverance, character; and character, hope. And hope does not put us to shame, because God's love has been poured out into our hearts through the Holy Spirit, who has been given to us.' Hallelujah! With that, we have all that we need in Christ Jesus.

Once we have developed this patience (or forbearance), grace and mercy can and will begin to follow as expressions of that patience in our lives. We can wear our patience like a garland around our necks, to help us through challenging times. Just think of the difficult season we have been living through because of this COVID-19 virus. Look at how we as a nation, even as the world, have been handling it. I tell you; this is a tough time. Domestic violence has increased with calls to the national domestic abuse charity helpline run by Refuge increasing by 60%. Think of the suffering of the women and children – and yes, sometimes the men too. We are not naturally people of patience.

Some situations demand extreme patience from us. Think of living with an alcoholic partner throughout this lockdown. Think of twenty or thirty years of living with an alcoholic partner, and you are a child of God. You desire to live for God with a sincere heart in this time of pandemic while your partner desires only to drink alcohol. How can anyone possibly cope living like that? The only answer is to dig deep into Christ Jesus and persevere.

We already know from our verses from Romans that suffering produces perseverance, which the author Paul knows only too well. Following his example, throughout our suffering we must continue to love one another and show it through out actions. Love has to be seen in sincere caring, not just talked about or written in poems. Let us reflect on God's love and patience now.

Reflection

Give God the praise he deserves each day and thank him for all he has done for you. Remember, as he has his eye on the sparrows, so too he watches over you. Ask him with confidence to carry you through each day with love, grace and mercy. You will come through these rough passages in life, and in doing so you will develop the gift of patience born from the Holy Spirit. Accept the joy of the Lord as your strength, ask him to build you up when you are weak and guide you through life's storm one step at a time. With his help, you will come through.

19

ISAIAH THE GREAT PROPHET
(ISAIAH 12:1-5)

When we began to enjoy the knowledge of Christ Jesus in our lives, we began to feel so different. We walk around saying 'Praise the Lord!' even if sometimes it just flows from our mouths. What a joy that is. Isaiah felt that too, when he started what became chapter 12 of his book with 'In that day you will say: "I will praise you, Lord"'. Even though what he wanted to write about was not easy, he started out with praise anyway. All through this book of Isaiah, the prophet continually reminds us of what God has done, even though he may be giving warnings to God's people, and sometimes even sharing sadness when he witnessed their behaviour before him. But whatever the situation, God's praises are always flowing from his lips.

The rest of Isaiah 12:1 goes on to say, 'Although you were angry with me, your anger has turned away and you have comforted me.' We know that God's anger doesn't last a lifetime as Psalm 30:5 assures us his anger only lasts for a moment. It may feel like a lifetime, as any amount of God's anger is too much to bear, but it truly is only a moment from him. Isaiah continues to reflect that God is his salvation and he will trust in him. Therefore he will not be afraid. The Lord will be his strength and his defence in his times of need, an example to us all these years later.

In verse 3, Isaiah encourages the reader that very soon they will draw water from the well of salvation. He did not include himself in this verse, moving from 'I' to 'you' in his speech. At this point he has begun to share his prophesies and doesn't know if he personally will see them come to pass; he is seeing these things in visions given to him by the Lord. In the timeline of the Bible, this passage is some hundreds of years before the coming of Christ our Lord, and it will be some 700 years until what Isaiah has seen will take place. He was not there, and neither were we. But we are now drawing the spiritual water from our Lord Jesus Christ who indeed is our salvation.

Isaiah says to us in verse 5, 'Sing to the Lord, for he has done glorious things.' I agree, the world should know what God has done in the past, but we should also be aware that in the here and now he is doing these marvellous things still. Many a time we pray for someone or something and we do not think we hear or see anything from God, sometimes for years, and many die without seeing their prayers answered at all. But I believe whether you see it or not, God does answer our prayers. I was told that when we see and hear the answers to our prayers, that is very special. Since we are asking different prayers for different things every day, we sometimes forget what we asked in the first place and do not realise all the things God has blessed us with, yet I know God answers prayer still. It is all about recognising his timing and ours.

Reflection

Some people think God spoke the Book of Isaiah himself; this is what I believe too. There are so many times the prophet speaks about the coming of Christ our Lord throughout the book, it must have come directly from God. For example, in Chapter 7:14 he tells us about the Virgin, who will later turn out to be Mary, Mother of Jesus.

Chapter 9 tells of Jesus' birth, the names he will be given and the awesome power he was going to have. In Chapter 11, Isaiah calls Jesus the 'stump of Jesse' and moves on to his crucifixion and resurrection in the latter part of the book. Everything he saw in his visions was accurate.

Isaiah lived to be 90 years old, or thereabouts, and there has been no prophet to rival him since. God knows this, so he still wants us to tell out the story of what Isaiah saw and said. We are called to rejoice and meet this well of water, our saviour and Lord Jesus.

We must sing to him and make his name known. We should also be aware that even though we have Jesus, we still have to keep on praising him and choosing to remain with him to stay holy (see Chapter 10).

Look again at Isaiah 6; even he thought he was holy, until he saw God in the temple, the angel put the burning coal on his lips, and he was cleansed anew. May God, the God of Isaiah, help us to seek, ask and knock unceasingly until we find him and remain holy in his presence.

20

A CALL TO INTERCEDE
(ISAIAH 33:13)

In the time of Isaiah, God despaired that no one was interceding for his people. Ezekiel 22:30 also recognises there was no one watching over the people of Israel. So, God did it himself. That saddens me.

In Isaiah 62:6, we are called to be watchmen, yet through Jesus Christ, God has established his own night watch. Do we understand the great honour which God has bestowed upon us, his people, in calling us to intercede for others and pray? He, the God of the universe, who created it with his breath, asks us, the children of sinful man, to intercede for others. We must remember that the closer we get to God, the more of a responsibility we have to hear and heed him. Only then can we truly understand his call on our lives.

We who draw close to God and live out his plans for us are living proof of Christ's call. Part of this call is to join him in interceding for others. We might think we are not able to do so. But every time we pray for someone, we are interceding. We can have every confidence God hears our prayer, even before we open our mouths. God knows our requests, whether he answers in a way we understand or not.

Paul the Apostle told the church at Ephesus he interceded for them every day (Ephesians 1:15-17). God also tells us how to pray in Isaiah, tenderly and in a comforting manner (Isaiah 40:1-2). If we remember the book of Job, his friends sit with him for a whole week before any of them speak, showing that sometimes we do not even have to say anything at all. Just be there with God's people.

As we learned during the time of lockdown caused by COVID-19 if we cannot go to see someone we can always keep in touch by telephone. Paul tells us in Corinthians 12 about the gifts of the Spirit. No matter what gift we have, it is through the Spirit. There are many different kinds of gifts working in different ways, but the same Spirit is responsible. So, there should be no more saying we cannot do things from a distance. There is always something you can do – but realistically we do need more than a hashtag on Twitter to thrive. We need our community, and we need God.

Reflection

If we believe in what we say we do, our life should be living proof. We should take everything to Jesus in prayer, knowing he will take it to God who promises answers. I know he is interceding for me even now! So, I can safely say my Hallelujah to him, as can all of us who believe him.

21

THE LOVE GOD HAS FOR US
(ISAIAH 41:8-15)

Throughout the book of Isaiah, there are many statements of love God makes to those of us who believe in his calling. In particular, from Isaiah 41:8-15, I focus on the following words:

> *'You are my servant':*
> *I have chosen you and have not rejected you.*
> *So do not fear, for I am with you;*
> *do not be dismayed, for I am your God.*
> *I will strengthen you and help you;*
> *I will uphold you with my righteous right hand.*

Well, if all these wonderful promises to us don't stay with you, then what will? They stay with me and sustain me through my darkest times. I have not got enough words to say to my God in return, only a grateful heart and songs of thanksgiving on my lips. I am in awe of the God who loves me so much, my father who loves me so intently. There is no way I can ever praise him enough.

Prayer

O God. Encourage us to buy into these words of promise. All those who wage war against us will surely be ashamed and disgraced. All those who oppose you will be nothing at all to us. It is absolutely wonderful for us, as your children, to have those words spoken to our hearts so plainly. May we personally receive all of these words the prophets spoke to us. Stir our souls to read the whole of this chapter and beyond, receiving other prophetic words of God given to us who truly believe.

1 Peter 1 reminds us of the Living Hope we had which is found in the acknowledgement of Christ Jesus living in us, and in God's great mercy. God has given us this hope by the birth, death and resurrection of Christ our Lord and Saviour, and has kept it in heaven for us where it will never perish. Hallelujah.

Amen.

22

THE LORD'S ARM HAS BEEN REVEALED (ISAIAH 52:10 & 53:1)

'The Lord will lay bare his holy arm in the sight of all the nations, and all the ends of the earth will see the salvation of our God.' (Isaiah 52:10). Let us explore what that means.

John 12:38 tells us that the arm of the Lord will be revealed, echoing the message Isaiah prophesies in Isaiah 53:1. Through his visions, Isaiah has already prophesied the Virgin carrying the Son of God (Isaiah 7:14) and declared the wondrousness of his birth (Isaiah 9:6). The Prophet also asked the question of who would be the messenger, sent ahead to carry the message about the revelation of the right arm of God (Isaiah 53:1)? All of these prophetic statements, 700 years before Jesus' birth, inform us God was already preparing to send his Son into the world.

Moses told the children of the Israelites that when he died, someone from among them would rise up to lead and guide them through life's journey (Deuteronomy

18:15). Consistently throughout the Old Testament, leaders and prophets were telling God's people the same thing, in different words and ways. For example, Isaiah 40:3-9 prophesied the coming of John the Baptist, preparing the way for Jesus. Yet they were all sharing the same news right up to the time of Isaiah. We were like sheep without a shepherd, completely lost. But God our Creator wanted his people to come back to him, as he does today. Despite his clear guidance, all the leaders and prophets did not succeed in shepherding his people well, as our Lord Jesus accused them through the Parable of the Talents (Mark 12:1-12). One of the reasons Jesus came into the world is to bring us back to God the Creator.

Jesus is recorded as stating 'And I, when I am lifted up from the earth, will draw all people to myself.' (John 12:31). In this, he is predicting his death. We know Jesus has been lifted up on the cross. In following him, we will be drawn back to God; that's the only way back to him. There is no other way. God even told Isaiah in chapter 51, verses 5-6, that his salvation is speedily on his way. The death of Jesus salvaged us from who we were, raising us up to whom God wants us to be, by bringing his glorious Son to die, giving us that salvation.

Reflection

My righteousness draws near speedily,
my salvation is on the way,
and my arm will bring justice to the nations.
The islands will look to me
and wait in hope for my arm.

(Isaiah 51:5)

Isaiah 52, verse 10, has been fulfilled even today. As the eyes of all, look to Jesus, the arm of the Lord has been revealed to all who love him and believe in him. The Bible tells us the Lord has made salvation known and has revealed his righteousness to the nations, meaning he, God, remembers his love and faithfulness to Israel while extending salvation to all the ends of the earth through the service of John the Baptist and the sacrifice of his son, Jesus Christ.

Praise Father God. I thank you for giving us your son, your holy right arm. For the death of our Lord Jesus has brought us back to you, God. Praise be to God.

Amen.

*God's children have been promised that we will be strong, even through old age,
and able to soar like an eagle.*

23

POINTS OF PROPHECY

There are some key points of prophecy in the Old Testament of the Bible which point to the coming of Jesus Christ. I have already mentioned Deuteronomy 18:15 and Isaiah 9:6 in Chapter 22. Here are some other points to notice.

Prophecies about Jesus come from a number of voices. Numbers 24:17-19 gives us a prophecy of Balaam, a seer from the Moabites. His people were the enemies of the Israelites, yet God revealed the truth to him, and he gave a series of prophecies to King Balak telling of their salvation to come. Psalm 110:4, written by David, proclaims Jesus Christ will be a priest in the order of Melchizedek, claiming his right to the title 'Most High' held by the former Genesis priest who was also a king; Jesus would similarly be both high priest and king. Malachi forecasts one will come who will prepare the way, widely accepted as John the Baptist.

Therefore Isaiah, as the major Old Testament prophet, made many declarations about Jesus. One of his most famous passages is Isaiah 52:13-53:12, the passage known as the suffering servant. Additionally, Isaiah 2:3 assures us the one to come will teach us his ways so we can follow him. Isaiah 16:5 tells us a throne will be established and Isaiah 46:12-13 assures us his righteousness will draw near to us.

Jesus is described in various ways throughout the Books of the Prophets. These include as the Root of Jesse (Isaiah 11:10), a precious and tested cornerstone in Zion (Isaiah 28:60), a Man of sorrows (Isaiah 53:3), the restorer of what was broken (Isaiah 61:1-4) a righteous branch (Jeremiah 23:5) and the one whom they pierced (Zechariah 12:10).

A number of prophecies are made about Jesus' life which came to pass. These include Jacob foretelling Jesus will come from the line of Judah, one of his 12 sons (Genesis 49:10), the Virgin becoming with child (Isaiah 7:14), the king riding into Jerusalem on a donkey (Zechariah 9:9), the 30 pieces of silver (Zechariah 11:12) and Jesus' resurrection from the grave, remaining untouched from death or decay (Psalm 16:10).

All of these prophesies told of the coming of our Lord Jesus Christ and were fulfilled throughout his life.

24

TRUE FREEDOM COMES THROUGH FOLLOWING CHRIST (JEREMIAH 7:23-24)

Too much freedom isn't good for anyone. It can have drawbacks. Yet millions of people each year are fighting for their freedom. I say without freedom life can not only be enjoyed but enjoyable. Freedom is sometimes mistaken for liberty, but I think we have to be clear about the difference between the two. Some might say without freedom we cannot have liberty, but they are different things. Liberty is living without boundaries while freedom is living as you wish but within boundaries. For freedom to work, it must have limits. For instance, freedom fighters think they can do as they like or say as they like regardless of the consequences. They may even use this freedom to steal, murder, riot or even burn down towns and neighbourhoods, indulge in all sorts of things, and says it's all in the name of freedom. No, I don't think too much of that is good.

There should be someone to be accountable to when we have freedom in our lives. This freedom that one so craves is a responsibility too. It is one thing to be fighting wars for freedom in countries where people's rights are oppressed. But otherwise, I think it is all a big moral mess. If we consider the structure of creation, we'll see there's a season for everything, a time for everything under the sun and a purpose too. We have been given the privilege of seeing it all. So with respect and wisdom, we should not use this freedom without limits to serve ourselves. Jesus has given us freedom that is right and true, but which also comes with accountability to him; this kind of freedom does not lead to destruction, but to new life.

2 Corinthians 3 tells us '*Where the Spirit of the Lord is, there is freedom.*' Yes, we are called to join in that freedom, but not to indulge in the sinful way of our nature. Rather, we are challenged to use the freedom given to us by the Son of Man to serve each other in love; pure, clean and sincere. There are some biblical figures who use this freedom in a most unhealthy way and pay large consequences for it. King David uses this authority and power to seduce Bathsheba even though he knew she was married (2 Samuel 11). The rich young ruler wanted to keep his riches but gain righteousness also (Mark 10:17-27). Jesus talked about the prodigal son who took all his belongings only to get so low as to eat the pig's food (Luke 15:11-32). These characters misused their freedom because they rejected accountability and came into

disaster. It is only through accepting accountability with Christ Jesus we can find true freedom; whom the Son sets free is free indeed (John 8:36)!

I know some of us have a tendency to get into a desperate state. For example, those who use their freedom to end their own life because they think there is no other option for them. Some people are living in terrible conditions and would prefer to die than live; but these plans are totally against God's plan. Even when we know our actions are against God's plan, we often take them anyway because we claim our lives as our own, instead of recognising they were purchased by God with the blood of Jesus. We do as we like instead of what is best. I know this kind of freedom isn't good. Yet in spite of all that God loves us and will always welcome us back to his path.

The Word of God says 'Obey me, and I will be your God and you will be my people. Walk in obedience to all I command you, that it may go well with you.' (Jeremiah 7:23). Yes, we make mistakes. Sometimes some terrible ones too. But God in his infinite mercy makes a way always. His eyes are on the righteous and his ears are attentive to our prayer. So he is always ready to help when we make mistakes. Praise and thanks be to God for His great mercy and grace, remembering whom we are as God's chosen people, truly free. Yet we must be wise in how we use our freedom. May God help us to be wise, and not succumb to our foolish natures.

Prayer

Thank you, Heavenly Father, for the freedom given to us through your Son, Jesus Christ. Be pleased to help us respect the freedom your glorious Son Jesus has given us. Thank you Father for being the 'always' in our lives. Thank you for this indescribable gift that gives us true freedom from condemnation in you, as you put all our sins behind us and leave them in the past. Please help us to accept the blood of Christ Jesus which sets us free. Help us to enjoy living for you.

Amen.

25

A PROMISE TO RESTORE
(JEREMIAH 33:3)

Jeremiah 33:3 is known as the hotline to our God and Father. He created all things, we know that full well, but if we spend a little more time to read the rest of chapter 33 we see the father's promises to his children when we return to Him. They are awesome. So many times he says the words 'I will' in this chapter, and we know he does as he says he will. In verse 3, God says, 'Call to Me, and I will answer you, and show you great and mighty things you do not know.' Look at the gentleness coming from this verse to his pupil through his prophet. There is such regard for us from such a great and powerful God.

We have a promise that we can call the God who made the universe on a direct line, anytime, from any place, from any situation. What a father we have! He wants us to come to him so much, so we can enjoy the glorious riches he has in store for us. He also wants us to be strong and courageous so that we can be his hands and feet, a light to the world and an ambassador for him. We are his representatives to carry his fame and make his name known in the world. This is his desire for us, in spite of our rebellious ways.

Whatever we do in our lives, if we call on him, God will forgive us, cleanse us and make us presentable again. In Hosea 14:4, God tells us 'I will heal their waywardness and love them freely, for my anger has turned away from them.' He is a true father, commanding respect while also loving us with gentleness. Once he has made us clean of our sins, God wants us to tell of his goodness and love across all the nations of the world, so his name will be made known and more of his children will come to him through Jesus Christ. His salvation is the only way.

One look at the state of the world today and we can see how much we need salvation. I am writing this chapter in 2021 when the death toll from COVID-19 in England is over 150,000 people. Yet we know in spite of this terrible disease God hasn't turned away from us. If anything it is we who turn our backs, not him. Not this God and Father. Not our Lord Jesus Christ. He has not forgotten his promises to us. It is us, so rebellious in nature we forget who we are; children of God. As we get rich and powerful, building our lives in our own ways, we think we have everything in our own right and we don't need God anymore. Yet we are very wrong.

In this time when COVID-19 is still very widespread, natural disasters keep on happening in country after country, forests are burning and heavy rain is disrupting, even destroying, cities and towns, we need God more than ever. Yet we are not calling upon him. Is it because we are ashamed of our behaviour? Is it because we have become so rich and powerful we think all this is going to pass, we can replace property we have lost, so we still don't need God? I say we are wrong if we think like this. What is happening in the world is the biggest of sorrows, and too late shall be our awful cry when we finally turn to the Lord.

Yet, God is still God. However we look at the state of the world, God remains true to his promises, and he will always be here longing to show mercy. He never tires of showing how far he will go for us. He even came down in the form of the man Jesus, to take up all that we even refuse to give; our sin, our shame and our disgrace. He allowed our faults to be nailed on a wooden cross, with great big nails driven in his hands. He accepted the stretching of his hands until his chest nearly broke, and declared to all of us 'This is how much I love you'. Good, bad or indifferent, the same love for you. This is the God who still promises to restore (see Chapter 23). All he asks you to do is to return to him with humble adoration. May the God and father of our Lord Jesus Christ help us to listen to his calling and obey.

Prayer

Two Chronicles 7:14 tells us God is still waiting for us to call him on that hotline of prayer. He will always answer. So let us pray to him now.

Oh Lord, do we need your healing hand upon our land? We do, so badly. Only you alone know how much, Lord. I cannot begin to tell you how this time of pandemic has humbled me. I pray, O Lord, that you will use it to return many hearts all over the world to you. We need you so much, Lord. We need you to heal our churches, schools, politics, families, communities and friends. We need you to save our lands far and wide, where there are so many disturbances.

Lord, we need you. I still cry out to you. I ask you to have mercy upon us, in spite of everything we do to reject you. Forgive us, O Lord. In Jesus' name. Amen.

26

LAMENTATIONS 2:11

Jeremiah lamented over Israel, so he became known as the weeping prophet. In Lamentations 2:11, he declares his heart is poured out on the ground because Jerusalem and her community of people have been destroyed. I am sure we all have something that is tearing our hearts out at this particular time. What might that be for you? Energy bills are rising with many people worried about how to pay for everything in their homes. That is not good, of course not. But is it worth pouring your heart out in grief as Jeremiah did? I personally made vows to the Lord that I would remain faithful to his ways. So, what does that mean for me, and those like me, in times of trouble?

In Matthew 5:4, Jesus tells us 'Blessed are those who mourn'. Yet if we live in him, what do we have to mourn about? Also, if we are the light of the world (Matthew 5:14), are we lighting up anyone's path by mourning – including a bereaved family? Are we also the salt of the earth, as we are called to be (Matthew 5:13)? How are we doing? Are we seasoning anyone's life? When we say yes to Jesus, and agree to follow him, these are the things we sign up for. These are the vows we make to God. David taught we ought to fulfil the vows we made, thus remaining faithful to God (Psalm 76:11). We cannot abandon them in times of sadness.

One thing we, as God's children, should be mourning is the lost generation of today. This generation has no desire to know God and embrace his wisdom. That may be our fault for the way have raised the children. The Bible does warn some will bring disgrace to us as people have throughout the ages. However, it may be true that we did not always do the right thing as parents, for example not introducing our children to Sunday school. But there are so many voices in society these days screaming in their ears that even those who were brought up in the church are being dragged away. Proverbs 1:20 says wisdom calls aloud in the street and raises her voice in the public squares. We can tell our children as loudly as we like, but they are not listening. However, we must go on telling them the truth about desiring knowledge of God. This is what should be on our hearts and in our vows to God. That is how we ought to fulfil our promises and be faithful to God. Our Lord would be pleased.

Reflection

Here are some words of wisdom to help us as we seek to remain faithful to God.

'Walk with the wise and become wise, for a companion of fools suffers harm.'

(Proverbs 13:20)

'The grass withers and the flowers fall, but the word of our God endures forever.'

(Isaiah 40:8)

'Those who walk uprightly enter into peace; they find rest as they lie in death.'

(Isaiah 57:2)

'For no word from God will ever fail'

(Luke 1:37)
– The Angel of the Lord, Gabriel, speaking

'Whoever does not honour the Son does not honour the Father who sent Him.'

(John 5:23)

This beautiful shrub needs care – just as the Lord does for us

27

GOD DEMANDS PRAISE (JONAH)

The story of Jonah is a very familiar Bible story to most of us. As the story goes, Jonah was running away after God sent him to warn the Ninevites to repent, otherwise, God would take vengeance. The Lord sent him one way, so Jonah went the other! He thought maybe he could trick God, something we often try to do. He even went to the bottom of the boat, thinking he could hide. Did he read the psalm that David wrote, asking the question: Where can I hide from you? (Psalm 139:7-12) The answer is, we cannot hide from God.

God whipped up a raging storm which threatened the boat Jonah was in. Jonah realised his mistake and let the sailors throw him overboard, so that the ship could escape into calmer seas. But God did not let him drown. He sent a large fish, maybe a whale, to swallow him up, carry him to shore and spit him out after three days and three nights. Is God not amazing? We too often underestimate God's plan. His messenger had a job to do, and nothing was going to get in the way. So, God sent Jonah for a second time to do his work in Nineveh, that wicked city.

Reflecting on this story gave me a little glimpse of hope for the difficult times we are in now. Even when we think things are bad where we are, sometimes we just need to stay there. Let God work out his purposes with us where we are. During the storm in our story, it is interesting to notice that the sailors who did not believe in Jonah's God had a belief in something. Jonah 1:5 tells us they called on their own gods, but nothing happened. So, they talked together, went to wake up Jonah and told him to call upon his God. Maybe he would take notice and save them from certain death? They could not yet see who was responsible for the calamity they were in. So, you see, my friends, the sailors knew it was not an ordinary storm. Sailors usually found out about the weather before they set sail; they had not expected that kind of danger. In desperation, they cast lots to find the cause of the storm, and the lot fell on Jonah. Once he told them that he worshipped the God of creation, the sailors who had Gods of their own were terrified.

Meanwhile, the sea got even worse, so the sailors asked Jonah 'What should we do with you?'

'Throw me overboard', Jonah replied.

I assume he knew this would mean certain death, and he wanted this as an escape. However, they did not throw him overboard straight away, instead trying to turn back as fear came upon them. Yet eventually, there became no other choice. The sailors had to call upon Jonah's God and acknowledge him, as they made their sacrifices and vows to him for the sake of their lives (Jonah 1:14). The fear of God overpowered them. I believe God requires praise and praise he shall have.

This fear of God is lacking in the world today. There is no fear of God, no respect for God. We think we can do and say what we like. When I say God is the same today as he was in Jonah's day, as he was in the beginning and shall be forever, it is the truth. He is still the awesome God. He is to be feared and respected. The God we worship today is the God Jonah worshipped, and the God the sailors feared. He is the same God who provided the fish to catch Jonah and bring him back to resume his mission. Only this time in obedience.

God demands obedience from us. That's what he really wants, and he will get it if he pursues it. We see through the story of Jonah he will do anything to fulfil his purposes, even using animals in mysterious ways! In this instance, he uses a fish, in Numbers 21:6 he uses evil snakes in the wilderness and in Numbers 22:21-31 he uses a donkey. Jesus told us that even a stone can bring praise to him (Luke 19:40). God demands praise and he is worthy of it.

When Jonah cried out to God from the belly of the fish, praising him and asking for help, God heard him and answered his prayer. The fish vomited Jonah out and he got another chance. God is a God of a million chances, and he continues to bless us with them. But I ask you, must we go on doing this to our God who is our father? We should thank our heavenly father for giving us that second chance over and over again.

Reflection

Isaiah 43:20-25 describes the rejection God felt when Israel had turned its back on him. Now, I find this really very sad even though at the same time I know it is true of us today. All God wants from us is our obedience. In Isaiah 45:19, the Lord says he did not tell us to leave Egypt in vain. For us, Egypt is wherever we were before God called us into his righteousness. He has a plan for each of us just as he had for Jonah, and he will do whatever is necessary to bring them to fruition. Let us look again at our lives and truly give God the praise he demands and deserves, thanking him for everything he has done for us.

28

DAVID AND JACOB

David and Jacob were two great servants of God. They both did great, great exploits in his name. Jacob was the father of the 12 tribes of Israel. Remember God changed Jacob's name to Israel after they had wrestled for a night by the river (see Chapter 7). David was a shepherd, warrior and King of God's people, the Israelites. Two great leaders chosen by God. They were born leaders even though they were very different in nature. Jacob was very cunning and mean, while David was very humble and God fearing. Jacob's name means a deceiver. The Bible says Jacob came out of his mother's womb grabbing his brother's heel, which is why he was called Jacob (Genesis 25:26). The rest of his story is played out throughout the rest of Genesis with his brother Esau, his mother Rebecca, father Isaac, his wives and many sons of later importance.

Jacob's life was not what we would call pleasant. We human beings would not choose him to pick a child up from school! But God who knew him before he was born knew all about him and chose him still. He was destined to be whom he became. He was Abraham's grandson. So that alone put him in a good place with God. He was part of God as a descendant of Abraham, a friend of God. Great things were expected of him, and not through his mother or father's choice as you see through the story. Gods plans and ours are often two different ways until we learn to follow his.

Jacob whined and stole his way through life until God was ready to use him. At the final point of wrestling with his future, God broke Jacob's hip (Genesis 32:22-31). That is when Jacob's life changed forever because he walked with a limp from then on. Sometimes it takes something drastic for God to get our attention. Jacob did not acknowledge God as his God. So, when he mentioned God, he called him my father's God. He lived life in the fast lane where he wanted everything yesterday and he did not care who got hurt on the way. Yet he was still God's choice to build a nation.

A lot of us are like Jacob. We want God but in our own way. We will not yield to God's ways even though he has the best in store for us. We will pray enough to him, but we will not let him have his way with us. We sometimes hinder God's plan or delay it. But however long it takes, God will have his way in the end. By not allowing God to have his way in the first place we do more harm than good to ourselves. That was Jacob. However once Jacob stopped wrestling, he went on to be Israel, the father of the 12 tribes of Israel, anointed as such by God. We can all learn something from his story.

Now for David. David was a humble person who knew God from an early age. I believe our upbringing can play an important part in our later years, and that David's parents have played a good part in his life. We do not hear much of mothers in the Bible, but when Saul was chasing him and David was in Misbah, he asked the Moabite King to let his mother and father stay there until David learned from the Lord what his will for him was (1 Samuel 22:3). So, it's not only Jesse, David's father who was named but his mother in his life too. We know he had seven older brothers (1 Samuel 16:10) some of whom were in the army (1 Samuel 17:13) while David was keeping sheep. While David was going backwards and forwards, looking after the sheep, the Lord observed his spirit and mind and was pleased. That's God; he doesn't favour our looks, size or education. He observes the attitude of our hearts.

David was young and brave, not big in size, but just the person God wanted to use. He looked after sheep well, the Lord recognised, so he would look after people well too (2 Samuel 7:8). David soon acknowledged God's calling on his life when Samuel came to anoint him (1 Samuel 16:13). Jesus told us in John 15:16 that we did not choose him, he chooses us, and here is an Old Testament example of exactly this. While Jacob lived life in the fast lane and did not find time for God, David knew God was everywhere. Unlike

Jacob who did not know God was seeing everything he did, David was building a relationship with God. Samuel called David a man after God's own heart (1 Samuel 13:14). Can God say this of us?

David was anointed king some 25 years before he got to sit on the king's throne, as Saul was still alive. I wonder sometimes why God had him anointed so long before he became king? Well, here I am writing a book some 30 years since I said yes to God. Sometimes we need to mature. David did not just sit there doing nothing, grumbling 'I don't know why God won't use me after he had Samuel anoint me!' He got on with living for God. He slew Goliath and helped out the people unhappy with the government. He looked after them. He said many times in the psalms 'I will wait upon the Lord'. He did become king and ruler of Israel for 40 years, fulfilling God's plan for his life. He ruled with dignity and turned the hearts of the Israelites to God. Job done.

Yes, David made some mistakes like all of us, but he allowed God to work through him also. The Bible points to David's great mistakes but the most important thing is that in Psalm 51, he confesses his faults to God and God has forgiven him. Yes, there were consequences, but such are the penalties for a humble and contrite heart. That is what God desires. That is what God is seeking from all of us. Both David and Jacob went on to serve God with contrite hearts and sins forgiven.

Reflection

May we read and consider the story of these two men, asking where we are before God our maker. We too are chosen people. God knows each one of us, but do we know him? Are we living life in the fast lane like Jacob, or are we walking with humbleness like David? These stories are not just there to fill the Bible. They are very strong stuff. They are for God's children to read and follow. Some of the written words in the Bible are there because God told men to write them on a scroll so that they may be left on record for future generations. They are for us.

29

THE LORD ALWAYS HEARS OUR PRAYERS

Psalm 81 is a perfect reminder that the Lord always hears our prayers (see Chapter 25). In verse 6, the psalmist reminds us God has removed our burdens and set our hands free. However, the psalm goes on to warn the people of Israel God will give them over to their wicked ways if they reject him. Romans 1:18 emphasises this is happening in the time of Paul, and I also think it is happening today. Yes, people get up to all sorts of things they should not do, so God gives us over to our selfish desires. God's people mingle with people of the world and bring down the wrath of God upon us all. If we think this pandemic of COVID-19 is bad, there is worse to come, since we have no intention of repenting or turning from our selfish ways.

As a wider church, we do not recognise the coming of the Son of Man as we should. Our leaders and priests are all ignorant. They are leading us down a pit of hopelessness. Our priests, pastors, bishops and even the Pope should be the tallest trees of Lebanon (Psalm 92:12). They are supposed to be those who are nearest to God. We know from Isaiah those closer to God must acknowledge his power (see Chapter 20), yet today those who should advocate for God and intercede on his behalf stand with the arrogant, the agnostic and those ignorant of his ways. As in Isaiah, God is looking for someone to stand in the gap and give counsel to his people (Isaiah 41:28). We are like sheep without a shepherd despite the spiritual leaders God has anointed. Why? Because they are corrupt and stand with the world, instead of standing up for Jesus with God's people who so very much need their help.

In spite of all this, our selfish ways and our waywardness, God is still standing at the door waiting to greet us when we come back to him. He will forgive our waywardness. He will heal our wounds, forgive our iniquities, give us grace and show mercy. He will take us back again. What a God we have. The word of God says whoever is wise let them heed these things (Hosea 14:9). Let them through their discerning understand that the way of the Lord is right. Let them walk in the ways of righteousness. Let them be us.

Reflection

24 The Lord Almighty has sworn,
'Surely, as I have planned, so it will be,
 and as I have purposed, so it will happen.'

(Isaiah14:24)

The Bible is the Word of God. It is the truth, and whatever one may say about it, it stands stationary and unmovable. Even though man may fail, none of the Lord's promises will ever fail (1 Kings 8:56). His words will come forth as they are settled in heaven (Psalm 119:89). He promises to always hear our prayers, therefore I know this will happen.

30

A PRAYER FOR STRENGTH

You, our God, are the strength of your people. You are our fortress and our salvation. You are indeed our father and our God. We worship and adore you. Great and mighty God, you are so awesome. You are mighty and wonderful. I love you Father, Son and Holy Spirit. You are so merciful and compassionate. That's why we worship you, dear Father.

You are the great God who created the hills and the valleys, the mountains and the desert. You send the rain on the entirety of the Earth, the North and the South, the East and the West. I praise you and honour you, mighty God. I thank you for the many blessings you bestow upon us, the children of men. I thank you for our Lord Jesus Christ. I thank you beyond words for the glorious son you gave to us, the children of men, to call us back to you. I thank you for these wonderful gifts of salvation and redemption you have blessed with us with.

Recognising your wondrous ways, Holy Father, I am pleading for your mercy, that this intercessory prayer be looked upon with favour and answered.

Holy God, our children are the children you've given us. We are your children, so our children are yours as well. I bring them to you in this, my prayer, today. I ask you to look down on the youth of today. Children are killing children. The evil spirits of the devil are throwing them into confusion, luring them into the habits of nicotine and alcohol; thus they are not in full control of themselves and have cause to kill each other. Holy Father, be pleased to look with favour upon us and come to our aid. Give us strength as parents, and as a nation, to intervene in the lives and situations around us and our children. Holy Father, be pleased to intervene, I pray.

Holy God, I pray for other nations in need. I particularly think of India, Pakistan, Afghanistan, America and all the Islamic nations. Dear Lord, I ask you today to introduce your glorious and wonderful son Jesus Christ to all these nations and peoples that those who choose to follow your way may have the opportunity to find you. This is my earnest prayer. Be pleased, Oh Lord, to enter into the lives of the rulers of these nations. Reveal your son to them, break the chains of oppression and indoctrination which currently rule their lives. O Lord, some have never heard the teachings of your glorious Son Jesus Christ. Others do not want to know. Please, Lord, look with favour upon my prayer and answer according to your promises.

Holy God, I acknowledge your son as the Prince of Peace. He is the only one who can bring the world to a place where we all can live in harmony and enjoy your wonderful creation. You, O Lord, are the God of grace, mercy and truth. Equip me to continue the work you started in the world. Convict me, O God, convince me and convert me to your own ways. Strengthen me where you know I am weak. Fulfil these requests, made by your faithful servant, I pray.

Holy God, I pray for this country, England, and its leaders. May you grant them wisdom and understanding. Lead them into the path of truth and goodwill. As your cleansing waters wash over your people, may you allow them to wash over the land. Be pleased to bless the churches and their leaders also. Grant them wisdom and the spirit of discernment, that they too may see, hear and understand what you want them to do.

Holy Father, be pleased to answer this prayer. I know you hear it and thank you for hearing it. I pray for the strength to remain faithful, continue serving and keep praying in spite of the challenges I face every day,

Lord. Thank you for all these things you are going to do, in the name of the one above all names, Jesus Christ, our saviour and king.

Amen.

31

PSALMS OF WORSHIP
(PSALM 98:1-2)

The Word of God says, 'Sing to the Lord a new song, for he has done marvellous things.' (Psalm 98:1) This is so direct. We read the psalms day in and day out. But do we stop and think of the marvellous things God has done, and is still doing? The writer of this psalm was David, who we know was a man after God's own heart (see Chapter 28).

I feel like David was spirit-filled when he wrote the psalms. For example when he wrote such words as these, 'When I consider your heavens, the work of your fingers, the moon and the stars, which you have set in places, what is mankind that you are mindful of them[?]' (Psalm 8:3-4). David's heart rejoiced so much that he just had to stop and worship God.

Of course, no one can ever tell of all the wonderful and marvellous things God has done in our lives. For one thing, the closer you get to him the sweeter he is to you. David writes that God's name is like honey on his lips (Psalm 119:103). I can believe that is so, for sometimes when a verse jumps out at me it can be like the first time I have ever seen it, and I cannot hold back from worshipping God myself. I felt like that when reading Psalm 98 during the height of the COVID-19 pandemic, and I do not think God was speaking to me about the Old Testament at that point. The Holy Spirit uses the scriptures to speak into our lives today, and I think that was what happened when I read this psalm.

If we do look back at the Old Testament, it is certain God has done great and marvellous things. Some deeds are so incredible, like the deliverance of his people out of slavery, whom he then takes for his inheritance. Millions of people along with all their livestock and belongings just got up and started emigrating out. All of a sudden, a whole nation. They did not even know where they were going. They had to be led, trusting in God. Amazing. He opened the sea for them! How awesome is that? That is only one of the marvellous things recorded throughout the Bible. So, I do not think the Holy Spirit is just drawing our attention to things in the past. I think it is encouraging us to look at miracles in the here and now.

I believe we need to focus our prayers and attention on the here and now, especially in this time of pandemic, political troubles and financial worries. In spite of everything, God has his plan. Nothing is uncertain to him. When David wrote in his psalms of the marvellous things of God, he did not even know about Jesus the Messiah, yet his coming was planned from the point of creation as the greatest work of God for mankind. God's holy right arm has worked salvation for him. Consider the wisdom of God; how wise how great, how awesome is he? As I am writing this, I have yet to know the marvellous things God has in store for the here and now, and for the future. What wonders may come to pass!

Reflection

Let us consider the marvellous deeds of the Lord in the here and now. For example, in 2018 thirteen boys and their teacher got trapped by rising water in an underground cave in Thailand. I remember the heroic efforts undertaken to get them out, taking some weeks. While the world watched and prayed – including me. In 2010, a group of miners also got trapped underground in Chile. They spent twenty-one days down in the mine, yet with God's help they came out alive. In 2021, I wept before my television screen as the governments of the west sent vaccines to India, helping them in their hour of need as the COVID-19 pandemic wrought havoc. Was this not a miraculous event?

These are only three examples of the great works God is doing today, and surely even they are enough to cause all the people to praise him every morning. Each day is a new day! Yes, one we have never seen before. What wondrous things could we witness if we open our eyes to the Lord today?

32

HALLELUJAH! PRAISE THE LORD! (PSALM 111)

The writer of Psalm 111 started at this awesome worship song with a Hallelujah! Praise the Lord! It is such a gripping psalm, one which draws me back to the Lord time and time again. I can feel the heartbeat of the person who wrote it in the cadence of the words. I imagine the psalmist was overwhelmed with the Spirit and filled with the presence of God at the time of writing it. 'I will extol the Lord' he starts the psalm, 'with all my heart.' For his heart was surely full of the joy God brings when you are in his presence.

Yet where was the psalmist planning to extol the Lord? In the tabernacle, or temple, God's house? No, amongst the people! The word used is 'assembly', or as we would know it, congregation. Ordinary people like the psalmist, people who just want to be close to God and feel his presence. The writer of this psalm truly worshipped the Lord, reminding God of his great and wonderful works. They are pondered by all who delight in them, and God ought to be praised for what he has done. Psalm 111:3 says, 'Glorious and majestic are his deeds, and his righteousness endures forever.' That is true worship, reflecting on God's deeds and praising him for them. The psalmist is encouraging us to remember God's great words, wonders and compassion so they may sustain us, inspire us and focus our hearts and minds on worshipping our awesome God. All of us, not just our pastors and leaders.

Verse five of Psalm 111 reminds us God provides for everyone. The whole world looks to him, even though some do not worship him or show respect for him. Often we forget relationship is a two-way thing, and we only want to spend time with God when we want something out of him. Do we ever spend time remembering the good things he has done for us? Even a little? Especially we who have been born again. Do we remember his wonderful deeds of kindness that he does for us as a parent does for a child? Verse nine reminds us that most of all he provides redemption for everyone who will accept it. This means the just and the unjust, the saved and the seeking and the sure and the uncertain. Truly, he is an awesome God, and to him belong eternal prayers. His words were meant to last forever, and I am thankful we have them recorded to reflect on and learn from today.

Prayer

Lord Jesus, as I sit to read your words, and meditate on the goodness of your teachings, I remember all the glorious things which are spoken of you. I join my voice with all the saints throughout creation telling out our souls and speaking of the goodness of you, our God.

I thank you Father, Son, and Holy Spirit, that you have stirred my spirit in me to really focus my attention on this song of praise. I pray wholeheartedly you will do the same for others reading this, my book. May your holy presence be felt by anyone who reads it and may they be inspired to say glorious things, speaking of all the goodness the psalmist has written of.

Amen.

33

REJOICE IN THE LORD
(PSALM 119:111)

'Your statutes are my heritage forever; they are the joy of my heart.'

(Psalm 119:111)

Should we not be the happiest people on Earth? Those of us who are called by God, given to his son and blessed with the infilling of the Holy Spirit? We really ought to be rejoicing in the Lord always, as he is our redeemer and our saviour. He has redeemed us from the world and has set our spirits free. Yet we know it is not always easy to rejoice even if we have the heart of Christ Jesus. In the Bible, we do not see Jesus always rejoicing. In fact, we are told of times Jesus wept or even got angry! With so much sadness in the world today I cannot see anything to laugh about most of the time, but I am blessed to still find joy within myself.

Even though I am used to experiencing it, the zeal of the

Lord's house still sometimes confuses me. It certainly did in the height of lockdown, when I was so depressed at seeing the church door closed, yet I was still able to find hope in my Bible. Some people say I take life too seriously, and that may be true. But tell me, what is there to rejoice about in a world where we cannot worship together? We must find a way. If we are in Christ and have him in our boat (Mark 4:35-41), we can smile at any storm and yes, in spite of our circumstances, we must rejoice in the Lord. We must make the effort to rejoice in the Lord. For in doing so we will tend to our spirits well.

Paul, our brother, encourages us to rejoice in the Lord (Philippians 4:4). He says, 'Do not be anxious about anything, but in everything, by prayer and petition, with thanksgiving, present your requests to God'. We are thankful for his encouraging words, but we must think of the situation. Paul knew, just as our Lord knows, that there are a lot of things out there in the world which give us cause to be sad. Especially if our heart is like that of Jesus, and we have earnestly prayed for our heart to be broken by that which breaks his. It becomes even harder to rejoice.

Why should we rejoice when the rich countries of the world are hanging on to vaccines that they can buy, even giving it to their children, when the poorest countries of the world cannot get enough for their old folk? Tell me how can I rejoice then? How can I rejoice when Christians are being persecuted and killed for acknowledging Jesus as God's son, all over the world? Children are being kidnapped from schools in Nigeria and going missing; how can we still sing 'It is well with our soul'? How about the souls of the mothers and fathers of those kidnapped children? We should not forget those who cannot sing 'It is well' with them. Have we not promised the Lord to hold his people in our hearts and intercede for them? (see Chapter 20).

Pity has no power, but the Lord is our strength. We should not waste our tears on situations we cannot change, but we must turn to the Lord. When Jesus was carrying the cross, he saw the woman weeping for him and said, 'Daughters of Jerusalem, do not weep for me; weep for yourselves and for your children.' (Luke 23:28). He was warning them of the troubles to be had when God was laid aside. Yet if we place God at the centre of our lives and rejoice in him, we will gain strength through him and find a way to live well in spite of the pain around us. There will be no need to weep for our families because we will have God.

Philippians 4:6 tells us to live lives of joy and seek out what makes us joyful. Prior to this, in Philippians 3:7, Paul reminded us to consider everything as nothing in comparison to the knowledge of the all-surpassing greatness we find in Christ Jesus. Paul was so excited about knowing God through Christ Jesus it was inexpressible, and throughout his many letters he encourages us to join him in seeking and searching, getting to know Jesus in greater depth. I agree, there is nothing which compares to the knowledge of Christ in you and the hope of glory he brings. Indeed, I have also come to the conclusion that in all things and in all circumstances, we must rejoice in the Lord.

Reflection

Jesus told us we will rejoice when the time comes. He will give us joy that no one can take away. Until then we are called to be sad with those who are sad, rejoice with those who rejoice and live lives worthy of the four gospels. May God help us all to listen to his words through the reading of the Bible, as they bring joy to our hearts and open our eyes.

Part Two

GOSPELS

34

A PRAYER FOR GUIDANCE

Guide us, O thou great Redeemer, pilgrims through this barren land. Lord, we know that we are weak and that you are strong. Please uphold us, your children, who trust in you, with your strong and powerful hands. Remind us that we are fed by the bread of heaven, which we can eat until we want no more.

O merciful and wonderful Father. As I look at the chapter in this book on 'Calvary: Deepest Pain' and felt the suffering that you bore for the fallen race of Adam, I can only bow my heart and my soul to you in adoration, thanksgiving and praise. I find within myself a great desire to worship you more. Yet I don't know how to worship you more. I am reminded of the songwriter's words.

What can I give Him, poor as I am?
If I were a Shepherd, I would bring a Lamb.
If I were a Wise Man, I would do my part.
Yet what I can I give Him? Give my heart.

('In the Bleak Midwinter'
by Christina Rossetti and Gustav Holst)

I am saying to you now, my Lord, here is my heart. Please take and seal it for your courts above.

Almighty Father, you who has given your only begotten Son to die for the sins of this world and raised Him back to life for our justification. Grant us the desire to put away all thoughts of wickedness so that we may always serve you in pureness and truth. Through the merit of your same Son named Jesus Christ who has become our Lord.

Amen.

35

ABUNDANT PRAISE

We have so many reasons to give our God thanks and praise, not least for waking us each morning to see another day. We must know that every day is not the same. That is why we call them another day. I imagine a grand cupboard being opened and the Lord taking out another day each morning. As he does so, he comments 'This one is absolutely beautiful' and then 'That day is beautiful too'. The Lord God made all the days beautiful in their own way, just as the Lord has decorated each part of the world in different colours and designed every nation in their own unique styles. So let us accept and appreciate these days our Lord God has given us; let us rejoice and be glad in it (Psalm 118:24).

Unfortunately, I know there are people who feel they cannot rejoice for the day they have been given. For some, it feels like each day is the same, all the time, bringing difficulties and sadness. May the God and father of our Lord Jesus Christ assist us in our weak effort, as we remember all those who cannot rejoice for one reason or the other. We must intercede with God for them. But for those of us who can recognise the beauty in each new morning, let us rejoice and be glad for ourselves and for all those who will praise God on that day.

It is worth taking a look at what exactly it means to praise the Lord. The Lord demands praise, I honestly believe, so we should understand it. I think praise is exalting someone, to show adoration by telling them about themselves in a good and honourable way. Raising their feelings of expectation, making them feel good about themselves. To me, that is praise. So, with God and to God, we should be inspired to give him abundant praise because he is worthy of nothing less. We as human beings have much more to thank and praise the Lord for than just waking up each morning to see another day; much, much more. If we only stopped to think about it, we would soon be overwhelmed.

We have to give thanks and praise to the God who gave us his son to bring salvation to us. Who made right the wrong caused by Adam falling from grace in Eden. We, who are walking with the Lord must remember his goodness to us, if we want to allow what we hear from his Word to have an impression on us. We must read and consider it, meditate on it, esteem it and give it the space to influence our hearts. We must tell of Mary's abundant praise that was made into a hymn, known as the Magnificat (Luke 1:46-55). We must reflect on David's psalms giving his abundant praise.

We can begin by thanking and praising God for his saving grace and mercy. We can praise him that he spares our life to see this new day every day. He is due thanks and praise for giving us his glorious son as our saviour, Jesus Christ. We should thank him every day for choosing us to be saved, adopting us into his family and his inheritance. How about giving thanks and praising him for the many gifts he has lavished on us, such as his love, shown to us in kindness? We may wish to thank and praise God for the knowledge and wisdom he gave us to know of him, and the desire he instilled in us to want to know him as Father, Son and the Holy Spirit. We know all three act as one, and we name the Triune God as worthy of thanks and praise indeed. For it is the Triune God who brings salvation to us all.

We have so much of God's goodness in us, in our families and in our day-to-day lives. Every year come Easter we'll remember the terrible time God went through with his son as he watched him nailed to a wooden cross to bring us back to him and fill us with such goodness. May we as God's children bear these things in mind and give him the praise and honour which is due to God our Heavenly Father.

Reflection

46 And Mary said:
'My soul glorifies the Lord
47 and my spirit rejoices in God my Saviour,
48 for he has been mindful
of the humble state of his servant.
From now on all generations will call me blessed,
49 for the Mighty One has done great things for
me—holy is his name.
50 His mercy extends to those who fear him,
from generation to generation.
51 He has performed mighty deeds with his arm;
he has scattered those who are proud in their inmost
thoughts.
52 He has brought down rulers from their thrones
but has lifted up the humble.
53 He has filled the hungry with good things
but has sent the rich away empty.
54 He has helped his servant Israel,
remembering to be merciful
55 to Abraham and his descendants forever,
just as he promised our ancestors.'

(Luke 1:46-55)

36

JESUS CHRIST IS GOD (JOHN 1)

To state that Jesus Christ is God may perturb some but is of no offence to most; either because they do not believe it, so it does not matter, or they do believe it, so it very much does matter! In declaring Jesus as a deity, we are making the statement he is not a smaller version of God, or a separate, junior God. No, he is God the Almighty himself. He is the Alpha and the Omega, the beginning and the end, the first and the last. He said he would live among us because he is Emmanuel, God among us (John 1:1-18). In the person of Jesus Christ, this promise was realised in truth.

It is wise and right to be cautious about claims of divinity. The mind is a factory of idols, as we human beings are constantly trying to invent a God of some kind or another. We seek any kind of focus to serve our own purpose and satisfy the needs of our own accord – which is impossible. Since there is only one God, who is the creator of this universe, any other focus for worship is folly. God promised he would come and live with us here on Earth, and he did so in the person of Jesus as prophesied (see Chapter 23). Thereafter he stayed with us in the form of the Holy Spirit. So, we see God through the actions of Spirit-filled Christians, even though no one can see God face to face. He has indeed come to live with us human beings and resides with us still.

As Christians, we believe that Jesus will come again as promised. When he does, he will declare to us all the things he declared to the Samaritan woman in John 4, to the Jews in John 8:58, to the Pharisees in John 9:39 and in Luke 17:20-21. He will declare 'I am the First and the Last. I am the Living One; I was dead, and now look, I am alive and ever! And I hold the keys of death and Hades.' (Revelation 1:17-18). All of this I know may be strange or even offensive to those who don't know about God or have no interest in knowing about him. Therefore, those of us who do know and believe in the Bible account, must stand on our faith without harming anyone. We must believe in our Lord and saviour, that he is with us in the Holy Spirit and that he is God above all.

Prayer

Thank you, Heavenly Father, for opening up the narrowness of our minds so that we can see and hear what you are saying to us. Thank you for growing our faith and fulfilling your promises to us. We know that if we seek you with all our hearts, we shall find you. We can say with every confidence in Christ alone, our hope is found.

Amen.

37

PREPARE THE WAY FOR THE LORD (LUKE 3)

Everyone is on high alert, with an expectant feeling. Something is in the air. Well, why else did crowds of people turn up to be baptised? They were stirred by something. Jesus had not started his earthly mission yet, but the kingdom of God was nearby. God with us, Emmanuel, was close. God did tell his prophets Isaiah, Jeremiah, Moses and even the smaller prophets that he would come to live among us. So, I believe the atmosphere was filled with something; anticipation maybe, hope almost certainly. I believe the Jews were, as they still are, waiting for the Messiah.

The Samaritan woman Jesus met at the well (John 4) told him that she knew the Messiah would come and would reveal all things when he did. So, when John the Baptist came from the wilderness and asked the people at the Jordan River, 'Who warned you to flee from the coming wrath?' (Luke 3:7), I do not think they could answer that question. Knowledge and truth had not yet been revealed to them, they had no Bible study class, no baptism class to prepare them. They only want to be baptised. But as they were being baptised, John told them to go and produce fruit in keeping with repentance, and they knew what he meant. Yet, just as their hearts were true, their minds were not focused, and they did not know how to repent as John instructed. So, John told them how to go about it right then and there (John 3:10-14) and people were baptised in their hundreds.

What was it that gave those who were baptised the clear knowledge they had to change? In asking John what they must do, they gave a lesson to us all. We all must be changed after baptism. We can't just go about and say we are baptised. There must be differences. John instructs us to produce fruits, to show the change in our lives. We need to turn from whatever life we were living before baptism. acknowledge what our lifestyle was and turn away from the things God would not approve of. If you are not living a life which is pleasing to God, turn your life around. Let others see the difference in your life.

As more and more people were baptised, the talk of transformation must have filled the air. After so long under Roman oppression, the crowds were ready for change and their hearts were stirred. This man baptising them must be the long-awaited Messiah, who speaks so of repentance and reveals the ways of God? John had to tell them he was not the Messiah, but one sent to make clear the path. 'I baptise you with water. But one who is more powerful than I will come, the straps of whose sandals I am not worthy to untie.' (Luke 3:16), he tells them. He went on to describe the second baptism as one of Holy Spirit and fire. This first baptism was there to prepare the way for the Lord.

Nobody could have predicted the next part of the story. Jesus himself came along and asked to be baptised. What a sight to behold! All these people standing there did not know they were witnesses to God's promises being fulfilled there and then. It was not until later, after John the Baptist was murdered, Jesus began to speak about him. Jesus revealed to his disciples that John was more than just a prophet (Matthew 11:11). Then the people who were baptised by John came to understand why they were drawn to him, and to the banks of the river Jordan. He was more than a prophet. He was preparing the way for Jesus to complete his work in turn.

Reflection

May God help us to read these writings more often, so we may truly explore and understand the lessons they have to teach us. May we take note of what appears to us, inspires us and guides us. Let us take those things forward into our lives, so that we don't just stay readers of the Bible, but also doers of God's good works. May God help us all.
Amen.

38

SALT (MATTHEW 5:13)

Salt is a very good thing overall. It is pure and has healing properties. One of the best compliments anyone can give you is when they say you are the salt of the Earth. That's because it is one of the natural products of the Earth, made from the sun and the sea. It's as natural as can be!

Salt is more than just flavour for our taste buds and even though doctors now tell us not to eat too much, as it is bad for us, it used to be a well-desired thing. Throughout history, people have even had their wages paid in salt!

Salt has always been more than seasoning for food. Job says a hard-boiled egg is totally uninspired without salt (Job 6:6) and I say that of porridge. Salt is also used as a cleanser to clean cuts and bruises and in storage used for preserving things. It is essential for life.

When our Lord told us we are the salt of the Earth, he was complimenting us. What a wonderful thing for our God to tell us we are the salt of the Earth! It has often been said of some of us but not with any sincerity. Jesus meant this of us in Matthew 5:13 with full sincerity I know. Yet he does go on to say salt can lose its flavour. I think he was warning us there is a risk of pollution in the world and from the world, that we can be corrupted and lose our natural purity. May God help us to remain as pure as fresh salt newly formed in salt lakes.

Salt is not always good, however. Salt stings open wounds. It's very good at cleaning them, but it stings. We should always be soothing with our words to avoid stinging others with them. A word should be soft and gentle; even our presence should be a treatment to a needy soul. Our kindness should be visible, and our actions like a balm. So, we must be gentle with our words and our deeds. Our encouragement should be pure and holy, clean and healthy. If we have wounded anyone physically or spiritually, we must try to make amends, gently, but truthfully. We are here to treat wounds, not deepen them.

Now just look at how our Lord Jesus handled the Pharisees in Luke 11:37-End. It sounds rough, but honest and truthful. That's the sting of salt. It hurts. Sometimes people need to feel the sting of salt to know they have wounds which need attention. Look at how Jesus answers Nicodemus (John 3:21). It takes guts from Nicodemus to stay any longer in the company of Jesus once the salt began to sting, but he stayed as he needed something more from him. The cleansing was worth the pain. Have another look at how our Lord handled his interaction with the Gentile woman in Mark 7:24-28. Even Jesus was a little harsh in this Bible passage, perhaps irritated or tired and responding to the loss of his quiet time. At least the Gentile woman was understanding. She was working hard to preserve the conversation so her daughter would get her healing.

Preserving relationships can be a real challenge spiritually. Often to do this you must go the extra mile for someone. You may know this person was in the wrong, or you did something wrong yourself, but it is more important to keep the spirit of love between sisters and brothers in Christ. We must do whatever it takes to preserve our relationship with each other. That may well mean we must swallow our pride, close the gate on whatever did happen and try to move on. We could minister to the person, get the person involved in something nice you are doing, bring back the smile on their face and the companionship between both of you. Remember, everything you do for them, you do for the Lord (Matthew 25:40). So even if it is hard to do it solely for them, give every effort to the Lord. Don't dwell on your difficulties. But do not get into the same position again; remember we who are of God do not fight against flesh and blood. We cleanse and heal.

Prayer

Lord God, we who are the salt of the Earth must learn to cleanse, heal and preserve the world around us, in Jesus' name. Help us to do this in all the different ways you call us to. God our Father, honour us in our work for you. Let our answers to our fellows be as graceful as can be, in every circumstance we face. Let us heal wounds, not harm. For God's sake.

Amen.

39

THE SERMON ON THE MOUNT (MATTHEW 5:17)

The law and the gospel are two faces of the same coin, which Jesus talks about in The Sermon on the Mount. We may try to fulfil the laws of God, and maybe we will be successful at some of them, at some point or the other. But Jesus, who knows all things, knows that it is impossible for us to always fulfil all the laws; that's why he came to do so for us. But where is our motivation? The law is a set of rules that we ought to be following, it is not the essence of how we should live.

God's motivation and the motivation behind his laws is to show mercy and love. This is the first and great commandment, to love the Lord your God with all your heart, soul and mind, and to love your neighbours as yourself (Matthew 22:37-39). So, this makes love the motivation of a Christian believer. God has shown us this love through his glorious son Jesus Christ, who is God with us here and now. That means all we need to succeed in love is right in front of us in Jesus. All that will satisfy God is found in him.

The Jews aim to satisfy God by trying to fulfil the laws in the Torah. I believe that is impossible, for the simple reason it carries a limit. God's love has no limit. God's love is unconditional. In Micah 6:8, we are told God desires us to love mercy, act justly and walk upright before him. How do we get to this place where we could live in this way? Joshua 1:7-8 encourages us to be courageous and focus on keeping all the laws. Yet as we can't succeed in this alone, Romans 10:4 tells us Christ is the culmination of the law, the end of it, so we can finally live in righteousness. In Christ alone our hope is found, the laws are fulfilled and the gospel of love is ready for all.

Reflection

'Do not think that I have come to abolish the Law or the Prophets; I have not come to abolish them but to fulfil them.'

(Matthew 5:17)

40

SEEKING JESUS: THE BEATITUDES (LUKE 6:20-23)

I n a recent reflection on Luke 2:49, where Jesus asked his parents why they were looking for him anywhere other than his father's house, the temple, I asked myself 'Why am I looking for God when I know I have already got him in my life?' I know people look to him for different reasons. So, I put the question to other people with similar mindsets while I was leading one of my Bible study groups. We came to the conclusion that we are still hungry and thirsty for his righteousness. That's why we were together in that study group. That's why whenever we heard that a group were going to meet and share something about Jesus, we wanted to be there. We just wanted to be where people were talking about him.

I never seem to get enough of talking or listening to someone talk about Jesus. I am still hungry and thirsty for the food that he provides. I'm not talking about filling our stomachs with natural food although he does provide for us in that way each day. No, I'm talking about the spiritual food we love to feed, our daily bread. We need to read or hear about all the things he has done and is still doing. In this day and time, we pray that he would do some of these things in the here and now, as we are going through such a terrible time with COVID-19. Yes, we need him to perform some miracles similar to those he did while he was here on Earth. The world is crying out for Jesus.

Take the case of the two men who received their sight in Jericho. They had a great need to find Jesus as they wanted to see (Matthew 20:29-34). What about the two men healed coming from the tombs by the Gadarenes seeking healing from mental illness (Matthew 8:28) Remember Jairus whose daughter Jesus raised from the dead (Mark 5:21-43)? They all had a great need to seek out Jesus. Many of us need to seek him out now in these days when mental health is at a crisis point for many and when the pandemic takes so much away from all of us. All over the world. We all have good reason to want to draw closer to God. Let us be bold enough to do so, remembering Jesus' words to us 'Blessed are those who hunger and thirst after righteousness, for they will be filled.'

Prayer

Thank you, Lord, for you are so great and merciful. You see us straining at the oars when the wind is rough and come to our aid. You have done so many wonderful things for us, as you did during your time on Earth and as you still do today. We are sorry that sometimes we use you for our own purposes; please forgive us. We just want to draw closer to you, spend more time with you and share more love with you. Help us to live our lives following the Beatitudes you gave us, for if we are hungry and thirsty for righteousness, they will give us succour. Let us take one step at a time with Jesus and he will fulfil our every need. We will be blessed.

Amen.

41

THE LORD'S PRAYER
(MATTHEW 6:5-6)

When Jesus' disciples asked him how to pray, the teaching he gave them is what we now know as The Lord's Prayer, or the Our Father in the Catholic tradition. I remember reading a quote from the great Scottish minister and writer William Barclay who said, 'We could easily sit in front of God with a sigh in our heart, as this prayer shouldn't be used lightly.' It is a powerful prayer which calls us to action.

The first thing we should understand is this is not a children's prayer – even though we teach it to them in schools. There is always a risk those saying the words won't understand the true meaning of them when they have such power and deserve such respect. Secondly, it is not for non-Christian people, as it is a prayer of one who desires to follow Christ Jesus by devoting their entire heart and life to him. Half-measures will not do with this prayer. You have to mean it all.

The prayer is set out in an orderly way across three stages. Firstly, Jesus reminds us the God of creation is our father, and even though he is omnipotent, his abode is in heaven. Secondly, he is holy, and he is to be worshipped by holding his name in the highest possible esteem. For holy is his name. Thirdly, we ought to think about ourselves and petition him for the necessities in life, such as the bread of heaven, forgiveness of sin and protection against the power of darkness. Thus, we are directed to bring the wholeness of the present, the past and the future before God in prayer.

The Lord's Prayer not only brings the whole of life into the presence of God, but it also brings the whole of God into the presence of our lives. When we ask for bread to sustain our lives, that request immediately directs our thoughts to God the Father who is our creator and sustainer of our lives. In asking forgiveness, we are acknowledging the direct authority of God in his son, Jesus Christ, our redeemer and saviour. When we ask for help to resist the future temptations that will come our way, that request immediately directs our thoughts to God in the Holy Spirit, our comforter and strength, our illuminator and guide, the guardian of our way ahead.

Therefore, in the most amazing way, this brief second part of the Lord's Prayer takes the present, the past and the future, the whole of human life, and presents everything as a whole to God the Father, God the Son and God the Holy Spirit. The Lord Jesus teaches us to bring the whole of life to the whole of God. The only way it can be considered a family prayer is if we offer it together as a Church family. Perhaps it should really be called The Disciples Prayer?

Reflection

Next time you pray using The Lord's Prayer, really take your time with it. Consider carefully the words you are praying to God. Do you really mean what you are saying with all of your heart? Are you truly laying the whole of your life before God and inviting him into the whole of your life?

42

THE NARROW GATE
(MATTHEW 7:13-14)

Which gate are you aiming for in life? I am taking the narrow gate. Jesus told us to choose the narrow gate, for there is too much distraction on the path to the wide gate with all that the world has to offer. Not a lot of people want to go on the narrow road to the narrow gate. They have a lot of baggage to carry with them, and it will not get through. Yet if we truly follow Jesus Christ, we do not need a lot of luggage. If we cast our burdens on him as he tells us to, we can walk freely with him on the narrow path. This is the way to sincere and long-lasting peace, something we all crave more of, I am sure. How can we have peace in our hearts if we are focused on the world and not God?

In Ezekiel 33:30-32, the prophet warned the Israelites against beautiful words with greedy hearts not focused on God. Jesus calls out the very same behaviour in Luke 13:22-28. Just as the path to travel is narrow, the gate to enter is narrow, and once it closes it will not open again however much one knocks against it. The owner of the house will say I don't know you, because even if you spend lots of time with God, if you don't show change in your actions, you will not pass through the narrow gate. If we say amen each time we hear his words, but still behave badly with other people, the gate will not open for us.

I have heard the story told of a woman driving her car with stickers promoting God all over the rear window, telling the world she's a Christian but when a car jumped her at the traffic lights the real person came out. She behaved so badly that a plain clothes police officer had to take her to the station and lock her up to calm down. In the end, she was kept overnight and then cautioned for her actions. We cannot just appear to be changed; we must show in our lives we are changed also.

Zaccheus proved he had changed instantly by confessing his sin there and then (Luke 19:8) and so should all of us. Godly sorrow leads to repentance (2 Corinthians: 7-10) and Isaiah 35 tells us there is joy in redemption. In taking the 'Way of Holiness' (v.8), we can enter Zion and be assured of our eternal glory. It is through our deeds that our worthiness to walk this path is secured. It's hard but it's so sweet, for Christ is with us. He is the best thing ever. Have you chosen which road you are going to take? If not, I'm encouraging you to choose well and choose the narrow way.

Prayer

God, I thank you for your promise to lead and guide us through our journey on this narrow path to the narrow gate. Without your help, Lord, we will not make it but with you all things are possible. Father God, please help us where we keep falling down. We acknowledge our weakness before you and ask you to give us your strength. Even the richest among us humble ourselves before your throne where grace and mercy are to be received. For it is through laying all worldly things at your feet we will enter through the narrow gate. Thank You, Lord, for hearing our prayer.

Amen.

43

WHAT IS ON GOD'S MIND NOW?
(MATTHEW 9:35-38)

What is on God's heart now in this time of COVID-19? Could it be he is looking down on the world and seeing the absolute misery and distress caused by this virus? So why are we not wearing him down with our prayers? Are we complacent as the Israelites were (Isaiah 43:22)? Yes, we are all still in pandemic times in the country, but we are too busy looking after ourselves. The shepherds do not see that the flocks God has given them to watch over have become hopeless and lost without them. Especially the old and frail who cannot or do not want to handle technology. They need their leaders.

John 4 records the walk our Lord Jesus took from Jericho to Samaria, to tell a woman there about the coming of the Messiah (see Chapter 44). She was the first evangelist, the first Jesus told to spread the news that he had indeed come, since the rest of Israel was not ready to share it. In John 4:35, Jesus declared the fields around him ripe for harvest even though traditionally there were four months left to wait. Jesus declared the time as right now and started gathering his people with the Samaritan woman.

Therefore, shepherds of the sheep and leaders of the people now is not the time to be so afraid to visit your flock. This is the time to be strong and courageous, to go in the strength God gave us. The world might say wait, but Jesus says 'Go'. He told us to ask for reapers to help bring in the harvest so that the sower and the reapers will rejoice together (John 4:36). All of us with different roles to play in this harvest can work together for the goodness of God. Those who are weak and frail, who were not allowed to go out during lockdown and may still feel safer shielding, should be encouraged to weary the Lord with prayer. They are not forgotten and there is a place for everyone in the Lord's harvest.

Still, the Lord says he looked for one to stand in the gap but there was no one (Ezekiel 22:30) and that brings tears to my eyes. We should have been standing in the gap and interceding for our people at all times. We must learn to weary him with our offences once again. Of course, there are lots of young people who are doing wonderful things for God, and I am thankful for them. I pray for God's protection of them. On people like the Street Pastors who sometimes even come to physical harm yet, they are out there doing God's work and caring for people. Praise the Lord for them. They truly are churches without walls. I pray for those who are called the Children of God, that they will make time to read our Bible every day and draw strength from the words of God on these dark days. May they take God's word into their own lives so this world might not be so dark for all of us. People such as these inspire me to step into the gap and intercede, so that God's mind may be focused on us always.

Prayer

Father in heaven, as I look at my reflections and writings, I give them to you now. You and I both know what is on my heart, Lord, but I would like to know what is on your heart. O God, I pray for your continued guidance and protection around me and my family while I seek your heart. Thank you for hearing me and my prayers. May you be pleased to add to the many blessings you have given me in my life. I ask this in Jesus' name.

Amen.

44

JESUS IN SAMARIA (JOHN 4)

The reason Jesus Christ came among us was to bring salvation to everyone, across the whole, wide world. I have come to seek out and find those who were lost, he said (Luke 19:10), not just to some of the people, but to all of them. Many will accept this act of salvation, but others will not. Jesus also says he has come so that we may have life and have it in full abundance, not just to exist but to live and live well (John 10:10).

The writer of Hebrews asked how can a person reject such a great salvation (Hebrews 2:3)? For some it is easy because accepting this great salvation means they will have to change, and they do not want to. For others it may be that they do not want someone telling them what to do, and they think that is what Christianity would mean. So they reject this great salvation. And in Jesus' case, he would be completely rejected in his lifetime, to the point of death on a cross.

The prologue to the Gospel of John states '[Jesus] came

to that which was his own, but his own did not receive him.' However, this was not the case when Jesus journeyed to Samaria. Since the Jews and the Samaritans were opposed to each other's ways, no one was going to tell the Samaritans that the long-awaited Messiah was here to offer them salvation. He was walking about in the world and doing wonderful things, but they did not know. Yet Jesus came for the world, not just the Jews.

Well, Jesus did go and reveal himself to the citizens of Samaria. The journey would have been very hard; it's all uphill from the Galilean area to Samaria. But Jesus did three days of steady travelling on foot to reach his destination, and what a harvest he received there! Not only did the famed woman at the well receive the good news of her salvation, but because of her evangelism, the whole community came out and met Jesus. It was the Samaritans who first knew Jesus as the Messiah while the Jews in Jerusalem did not know him at all. The Samaritans, whom they despised and rejected, saw the truth before the Jews. Isn't it funny how things turn around sometimes?

Reflection

Jesus had worked miracles before he went to Samaria (for example Mark 8) but he told those present not to share what had happened. The time had not yet come. Yet when he got to Samaria, he told the woman at the well to share the news of his arrival. Now Jesus has revealed himself, it is our duty to tell others about him, once we have found him. He told Mary Magdalene to go and tell his disciples (John 20:17), he told his disciples to go into all the world (Matthew 28:19) and now is it our turn. Yes, when our Lord revealed himself to all of us who believe, we must go on to tell of the greatness of our Lord. The joy of the Lord is our strength!

45

THE DOUBTING OF JOHN THE BAPTIST (MATTHEW 11:1-19)

John the Baptist asking if Jesus was the Messiah after God's anointing at his baptism may seem strange. God had proclaimed Jesus to be his son, after all. But in my view, John was right to seek clarification if he was not sure. I believe if you have a doubt about anything, and there is a way of clearing your doubt, then you should do it. In many ways, John was brave to send and ask the question. Maybe his patience was wearing a little thin, being cooped up in chains in prison. Maybe he saw his death coming and wanted to confirm his hope and belief in his heart. Whatever the reason, Jesus saw the goodness in it, and he did answer. He told John's disciple to go back and tell him what had been heard and seen, comparing him to Elijah as a mark of honour for all he had done.

John's teaching and preaching had been very different from Jesus'. John preached doom and gloom, anticipating a warrior Messiah who would strike the Roman oppressors down by raising an army – as many of the Jews did. Yet Jesus preached forgiveness and love. You can understand why doubts may have begun to creep in. How did that teaching align with overthrowing empires? In a strong lesson for those of us who look for revenge and wrath, Jesus never offered those things. He offered a new kingdom of love, peace and reconciliation. Those who look for those things will never be disappointed again.

Reflection

If someone asks us about Jesus' life and ours, his life-changing power, we tell him what he has done for us and they still have doubt, we ought to tell that person to have a go and ask Jesus into their own lives. Invite them to experience his life-changing power for themselves. The argument for Christ isn't an intellectual debate, is it? It's an experience of the life-changing power he wields.

46

A CALL TO FOLLOW
(MATTHEW 11:28-30)

There are always choices in life, between good and bad, or right and wrong. Just as there are choices between hot and cold, wet and dry, or black and white. There are also two rulers in the spiritual realm; the Creator of the Universe and the Power of Darkness, who tempts us to make poor choices. God in his infinite mercy gave us variety and allowed us to make choices, even though some of them are downright destructive.

God, in his great love for his creation, gave us a guide by which to make our choices by calling men and women of long ago, instructing them to record words of life and death in the Bible. This shows us the way as a constant reminder of how to live good, right and proper lives in this world he created. He chose prophets, priests, kings and judges and filled them with wisdom to demonstrate how to live a good life. But of course, sin entered the world through disobedience, which is all around us today.

Yet God, who created everything and knows everything, has plans for his creation. He knew that mortal man would soon wander away from him, even though he was our creator and father. His plan was that we should follow the lifestyle of the priests and kings and lawgivers he sent us as recorded in the Bible. This life is pleasing to him. But because of the Power of Darkness, even the prophets, priests and kings succumbed to sin and were unable to lead as they should (Isaiah 48:6-11).

So, God in his great mercy uses his righteous right arm in the form of his glorious son, Jesus Christ (Isaiah 51:5). All throughout the Old Testament the prophets, priests, kings and judges wrote about someone who would come to lead us back to God. All those who fall away, or those who refuse to follow would be shown a path back to him. God's glorious son stretched out his holy hands, calling us to follow him, even to death on a cross. Yet we are still stiff-necked. God has poured out his love, grace and mercy for us through Jesus, his only begotten son. Yet we are all foolish. Jesus came to show us how to live and love, be compassionate and merciful to each other, thus following him. But even that is hard for us.

God allowed Jesus to die for our sins. He died in pain for our sins, even though he had no sin of his own. In return, God only asks us to believe and trust in him for who he is. We should become believers in Jesus' awesome power given to him by God the Father who created the universe, that he would bring us back to God who created us for himself. Yet some of us rejected that free will of salvation Christ Jesus brings. Jesus invites us to follow him to the Father when he says, 'Come to me, all you who are weary and burdened, and I will give you rest. Take my yoke upon you and learn from me, for I am gentle and humble in heart, and you will find rest for your souls. For my yoke is easy and my burden is light.' (Matthew 11:28-30). 'I am the way and the truth and the life. No one comes to the Father except through me.' (John 14:6). There is no other way. No other choice.

So, if we acknowledge that we've sinned against God and man and want to make amends, we have to do so through Jesus Christ; for no one can go to the Father except through Jesus Christ who is Lord of all. And if we do not go to Jesus, who will we go to? Can we go through life carrying everything on our own? The weight of this world is far too hard for anyone to live in freedom without Christ Jesus in their life, it is not possible. You can go on trying to pretend you are happy when you are truthfully blue. You are not living, you are only existing. Life without Christ Jesus is nought. God sent His holy and righteous Son into the world to bring peace to our souls as the Prince of Peace and bring comfort to the comfortless, as he is the wonderful counsellor. No one, no, nothing can match him. He can close doors no one can open, and he can open doors no one can lock. Yet he will not force himself on you. He gave us free choice and free will. He showed us his hands, his path and the other paths. He gave us knowledge and told us to choose.

I hope today that we chose well.

Reflection

Hebrews 1:1-4

'In the past God spoke to our ancestors through the prophets at many times and in various ways, but in these last days he has spoken to us by his Son, whom he appointed heir of all things, and through whom also he made the universe. The Son is the radiance of God's glory and the exact representation of his being, sustaining all things by his powerful word. After he had provided purification for sins, he sat down at the right hand of the Majesty in heaven. So, he became as much superior to the angels as the name he has inherited is superior to theirs.'

47

JESUS' MOTHER & BROTHERS
(MARK 3:31-35)

t is staggering when you consider the crowd of people around Jesus when he visited Galilee, where he grew up. It was so busy that his mother and brothers could not get near him! When Jesus was walking amongst the crowds in the Galilean areas, people were drawn to him. There was a silk road running through the area bringing trade from the East, so access was easy. At that time, population estimates range between 150,000 – 300,000 people living in that area. It was a very popular place, a very different place from what it is now.

Jesus was like a popular film star of today. Even though the people did not really know who he was, they knew he was someone to be around. He had his disciples like bodyguards around him, and an entourage of supporters following him. So great crowds followed him wherever he went. It is no surprise his family found it difficult to see him. Yet here is the astounding part of the story. When someone told Jesus his mother and brother were looking for him and wanted to see him, he said, '*Who are my mother and my brothers?*' (Mark 3:33). Some translations of the Word of God state he pointed his finger at the people sitting around him, who were hanging on to every word he spoke. He went on to say 'Here are my mother and my brothers! Whoever does God's will is my brother and sister and mother.' (Mark 3:34). Wow. That must have hurt Mary and his siblings, but Jesus is always right. Who could argue with him?

It makes perfect sense that if we are all God's children, we are all brothers and sisters, so therefore we would be Jesus' brothers and sisters too. While I understand that is the message Jesus gives us in this Bible passage, out of respect for him I must confess I find it difficult to call Jesus my brother. Yes, he was the son of Mary, but also the son of God. He is righteous and holy and I am a wretched sinner. It is hard to accept but we are elevated to the family of God, says the Lord. If we truly believe what we read in this passage, we can come to no other conclusion as to how Jesus regards us. May we be bold in owning who we are out of respect for him. We are surely privileged people. We have been placed in very high esteem before God. We should act like it.

Reflection

What more can Jesus do for us to show us how beloved we are? He died for us. He rose from the dead through the awesome power and might of God the Father. He cleansed us with his blood and made us presentable to the father, so we may be truly embraced into the family of God. And when we mess up again, if we humble ourselves and go to him, he will cleanse us again. At times. he is ready and waiting for us even before we know we need him.

One day, we will stand before him and Jesus will hold out his hand to his father and say 'I died for this one, Father. I have prepared a place for her.' They will open wide the door and bid us to come in. Then we will see the river of peace. What else can I say? But wow.

48

JESUS USES SIMON PETER'S BOAT
(LUKE 5)

The boats along the shoreline were empty. The fishermen were washing their nets. There were people everywhere, as you would expect when the boats had just brought in a catch. Jesus wanted a little space from the crowd so his teaching could be heard better, so he borrowed a boat and moved a little way into the shallows. He taught the people from there. I think the fishermen were too captivated by Jesus to be annoyed by him.

After he had finished teaching, Jesus told Simon (as Peter was named then) to head for deeper waters and let out his nets. I imagine Simon Peter wanted to go home; the day was already late. It's what fishermen did when they finished their work for the night. Besides, he didn't know who this man, Jesus, was. The last thing he wanted to do was go back out fishing. Still, he did as Jesus asked him. When they reached the place Jesus told them to go and let down their nets, they caught so many fish, large ones at that, they had to call the others to come and help them! The two boats gathered so many fish they almost sank!

Simon Peter then realised this man was not an ordinary man. He fell to Jesus' knees in astonishment and begged him to leave in, knowing his own sinfulness and unworthiness. It was then that Jesus, our gracious Lord, called Simon Peter to follow him. He said, 'Don't be afraid; from now on you will fish for people.' At this, Simon Peter left everything and followed Christ Jesus for the rest of his life.

There are several lessons in this story for us, as Jesus followers, to understand and learn from. First of all, we have to be available for God to use us. Look what amazing things can happen when we let them! Sometimes, like Simon Peter, we may not feel like obeying God. Simon Peter had already worked all night. So, it was sheer obedience to God and a sense of calling in what he had just heard from Jesus which led him to set the boat out again. Things were never the same again for Simon Peter and his friends. Listen, obey and who knows what God may have in store for you.

Jesus will not break down any door to reach you unless you are physically ill or in danger. We must make ourselves available as Simon Peter did. His boat was available, and Simon Peter and his friends were washing their nets and therefore available. Revelation 3:20 pictures Jesus standing at the door outside, knocking, wanting you to open the door. He will not break it down; he will wait for your invitation. You must open the door before he will come in. Then Jesus will fill your heart with untold blessings.

Simon Peter did not keep Jesus' blessing for himself and his crew. No, he called for the neighbouring boat to come and share what God had blessed them with. Isn't that the way things ought to be? God blesses us so that we can be a blessing to others. Proverbs 11:25 reminds us that those who help others will be blessed in turn, and so the gifts of God to the world will be shared. If we Christians practice hospitality as we are called to do, we will give to the world as God intended. I always say when God blesses you with anything, you should share the gift, be it money, your house, your car, your testimony, his words, or good advice; share it all!

Simon Peter will never have forgotten that day when he came face to face with God. Like all of us, we remember how we get our calling, and whether we recognised it at first or not. God is always calling us, and those of us who are Christians did at some point answer our calling with faithfulness. We cannot please God on our own. So, by faith, we heard his words and by faith, we responded in order to learn how to please him through Jesus. John 15:16 says we did not choose God, but he chose us. Our choice was to invite Jesus into our hearts. So, we will praise God, learn from Jesus and, like Simon Peter, we will never forget that first day we took the risk of obedience to him.

Reflection

We all make mistakes from time to time, and none more so than Simon Peter. Yet God continued to use him throughout Jesus' life and beyond his death and resurrection, each time reinstating him back at a higher level and with more insight into himself. John 21:1-19 describes how Jesus even reinstated Simon Peter after his denials on the day of Jesus' trial. May we, as God's children, read the Bible more and more, understand that those people we read about were human just as we are and seek God's direction for how to be available to him, that as he uses us in whatever areas of our lives we might bear fruit for our Lord Jesus, our saviour and God.

49

ASK BIG AND BELIEVE – YOU SHALL RECEIVE (MARK 9:17-27)

I n this Bible passage, the father of a boy with seizures asked our Lord Jesus for help. He had seen the disciples previously, but no one had been able to offer relief. 'If you can help?' asked the father. 'If I can?' retorted Jesus! 'Everything is possible for one who believes.' (Mark 9:23).

Later, the disciples asked Jesus why they could not drive the evil spirit out of the boy. In those days, people believed seizures were caused by evil spirits, not understanding illnesses like epilepsy as we do today. Jesus' reply from verse 23 would indicate it is to do with a lack of faith. Yet Jesus says in response to the disciples this type of issue takes particular prayer (Mark 9:29). Well, is that so?

I think often about our faith when I read this story. Our faith isn't strong enough to do what we are called to do, yet we know that it is faith which makes us who we are in the first place. Jesus also tells us if our faith is as little as a mustard seed, we will be able to move mountains (Matthew

17:20). So do we have enough faith or not?

I think there are three different types of people in this world faith-wise. Firstly, there are people who think things will happen no matter how hard one tries, without rhyme or reason, and you will never know what is going to happen next. This is known as the Theory of Contingency. Followers of this theory believe everything is accidental, and all you can do about life is respond to what happens as it happens. Secondly, we have those who say life is hopeless, there is nothing on the other side and there is no God. They say the only thing guaranteed about life is death, so they are known as Fatalists. They believe what must be will be so there is no need to make any effort. Fatalism teaches that you cannot do anything about life. Thirdly, we have the Christian belief which teaches that there's resurrected life, so there is hope. If we believe, Christians have certainty about tomorrow. we believe life can take another direction if we ask God to guide it. It is never over until God says it is over. We also have faith in Christ Jesus, and as he told the disciples (and us!) in Mark 9:23, in him all things are possible. We only need to believe, ask and we shall receive.

Fundamentally, faith is believing in what we have not seen. Jesus tells the Canaanite woman she has much faith (Matthew 15:28). What did that woman do, except hold onto her faith that Jesus could heal her daughter even though Jesus tried to put her off? She affirmed her faith and secured healing for her daughter. Is that why we do not

181

get our healing even when we ask? Is it because we aren't affirming faith and pursuing Jesus as we ought to? Are we taking a fatalist attitude, or just adapting to contingency, instead of believing, asking and receiving?

I use the word 'belief' more and more these days because I have come to understand that is the most important thing for us. We cannot have lingering doubts. If we are not moving mountains, this will be the problem. I believe, like the children of Israel, we can see the bigger things which happen in our lives, but the little things we do not appreciate. God is still doing the big things every day in our lives. He is still protecting us from the enemy. He is still making a way for us in the wilderness. He is still the great provider, giving us the bread of heaven each day. He is still the awesome God who can divide the sea for us. We just need to believe in him. We need to ask for an increase in our faith. Our Lord Jesus tells us to ask, seek, knock and we shall receive (see Chapter 48). So let us get on and do what we ought to do. The Lord will help us. He is generous and faithful. He is, after all, our father as well as our God.

Prayer

Loving father, forgive our foolish ways. I pray that we will always remember to bring our troubles to you, so we can recover our rightful minds and serve you with pure lives. In deeper reverence, may we praise you, Lord. Thank you, father, for your gift of the Holy Spirit, with which you have opened the eyes of our mind and heart so we may have this blessed assurance of salvation. As I spend time with you in devotion each day, I thank you and praise you for being mindful of me, and letting your presence be known in my life. Thank you, Lord.

   Amen.

50

THE 'WOW' FACTOR
(LUKE 13:10-17)

We are not sure if the writer of The Gospel of Luke was a direct eyewitness to the works of our Lord. Some people think this book contains the words of Simon Peter, instructions he was putting down on paper for others to follow. Others think it is a collection of eyewitness testimonies put together in later years. Luke is a book to read slowly and take care of, for there is much to learn in it. My reason for reading this book slowly is that I really want to know more about Jesus, and there is much to be found here.

The last time I read this passage from Luke 13, a word came to me as I reflected on it, and that was 'Wow'. It is just how I felt when I considered what happened on that Sabbath. Then I realised these things are still happening today. We can see amazing things happening in the Old Testament. We can see amazing things happening in Jesus' days. They have always been happening. But sadly, we spend no time paying attention and staying amazed at the great and wonderful works of God.

Sometimes we hear or see something on the news that really deserves a 'wow'. I remember in 2019 when it took a surgeon 50 hours to separate twins that were joined at the head. There was another occasion in 2010 when, 28 days after an earthquake in Haiti, someone was pulled out alive. These are both examples of God still doing amazing work to this day. Even after flinging the stars into space and keeping them up. You think he would be finished after his work on creation! Yes, God is always doing amazing things.

Let us think about the healing of this poor lady in John 13 who had been bent over for eighteen years. Eighteen years is a long time to be in that position. But this one day was her day. Jesus physically touched her and she was healed. Remember at this time, Jesus was like a superstar walking among the people with his entourage of 12 disciples and hundreds following along all the time. How difficult it must have been for the older people who were there, to get close to Jesus and have their needs met. Yet this woman managed to do so.

Considering this is the miracle worker, the Son of God, I know this woman was healed. The Bible passage tells us she immediately straightened up. What a 'wow' moment that must have been! How about this; Jesus has prayed for us too! Doesn't that have the 'wow' factor? We have all had our one day when Jesus has passed by us (see Chapter 51), all of us who believe in his teaching. Perhaps some of us can remember when we were touched and told to straighten up by our Lord, perhaps others cannot. I can remember my moment, but I will not bore you with it. I do recognise, however, that I was bent over for more than 18 years spiritually. All of us, at one point or another have been bent over in a way. And yes, Jesus touches us to straighten us out. We are living proof that these things happen.

When was the last time we really saw a 'wow' moment in our own lives from God? I encourage you today to ask for the spirit of discernment. If we do, we will receive it, enabling us to see and understand God's will and purpose in our daily life. We will be able to stand in God's presence and enjoy Christ Jesus more. If we then ask the Lord to increase our faith, we may then be a blessing to more people who may be bent over in their lives as we were, even some of the people whom we have been praying for over a long period of time. Let us keep on praying for them since we never know when their 'one day' will come. Their 'wow' moment could be just around the corner.

Reflection

Mary Magdalene must have got the biggest 'wow' moment when she went to the tomb where Jesus was laid and did not find him there, only to hear him call her name (John 20:15). There are many, many more of these 'wow' moments in the three and a half years our Lord ministered on Earth. I encourage you to go back and read the Bible with more discernment. Let us not race through the pages to say how many times we've read the Bible from cover to cover. Make time to stand in awe of God from Genesis to Revelation. He is an awesome God, and he does awesome things. Let us not miss anything. Keep in touch with God and you will never want to put his Word down.

51

BLIND BARTIMAEUS
(LUKE 18:35-END)

In Chapter 15 of this book, I mentioned the story of Blind Bartimaeus. This story is told in three of the Gospels; Matthew 20:29-34, Mark 10:46-50 and Luke 18:35-End. Jesus was passing through Jericho when a man called Bartimaeus was sitting at the roadside begging, as he was blind and could not walk. He heard a noise or the commotion of a crowd coming up the street. So, he asked someone what was going on. Someone told him that Jesus of Nazareth was about to pass by.

Bartimaeus began to cry out, 'Jesus, Son of David, have mercy upon me!' (Luke 18:18). Why would he be crying out like that? It seems like Bartimaeus knew something of Jesus already. I believe he must have heard rumours of his great works. People tried to stop him and quieten him, but he would not remain silent, in fact he cried out all the more! He cried out until Jesus told his entourage to bring Bartimaeus over. Jesus could have gone on his way without listening or doing anything but that is just not who he was. He was a man of great compassion. He would not just pass Bartimaeus by, especially as Jesus already knew what his request would be.

So, when Jesus invited Bartimaeus to ask for what he wanted, the reply came, 'Lord, I want to see' (Luke 18:41.) We do not know how long Bartimaeus had been blind. The Bible does not say. At this point all we know is he wanted to see, which I believe he always craved – wouldn't you? Suppose he had been blind from his youth, or had been born blind, and had to live all through his life without sight. Now, through his encounter with Jesus, he would be seeing things he had never seen before, like the different shades of green, if he needed clean clothes or bedding, if he needed to wash mud off him or have a shave. It is too wonderful to imagine how Bartimaeus' life has been changed. Maybe he could now work and experience life quite differently. He was completely mentally, physically and spiritually changed.

We should all experience significant change when we meet Jesus. We know the devil doesn't want us to change and that's why the crowd in this story were telling Bartimaeus to be quiet. But we also know the devil is a deceiver, a loser. Therefore, we must affirm what we know of Jesus and his teachings to keep us focused on what we want. Bartimaeus knew what he wanted and did not let the crowd put him off. So I say to you today make every effort to get Jesus our Lord's attention. Be sure of what we really want from him, since he tells us to ask, seek, knock and we shall receive.

Jesus will hear and answer when we call, just as he did for Bartimaeus.

Reflection

Bartimaeus got what he wanted because he brought it to Jesus. It's never too late for us to cry out to our Lord for what we want as he will always make time for us. He will stop and listen to us, always. This leads me to ask the question, what do you want Jesus to do for you right now? Today? Imagine Jesus was coming near to you in person today. What would you say to him? What would you ask for? Why not take a minute or two in quiet and consider this now?

52

HEADLINE NEWS – THE LAZARUS STORY (JOHN 11)

The headlines today can be so depressing. Peace talks breaking down, leaders refusing to negotiate with each other, so many displaced people trying to seek asylum while governments find ways to not take responsibility for them. Daily death rates of over 150 from COVID-19 alone, and discussions about supply shortages due to Brexit and war. Protests, political upheaval and people not knowing how they are going to pay their bills. Floods and earthquakes, fires burning and every country dealing with so much pain and sadness. It is enough to drive anyone to despair, all this doom and gloom.

I am listening to the radio while writing this chapter and all I can hear is people calling in to the show, telling their stories of illness or terrible news, to impact their lives. But today I am bringing some good news. The knowledge of Jesus Christ is good news. Solomon, who was the wisest person ever, told us to get wisdom and get it at any cost

(Proverbs 4:7). Therefore get it, even if it costs all you have to do so. Gain understanding, for the fear of the Lord is the beginning of understanding (Proverbs 1:7). To seek Jesus is the greatest wisdom there is. Jesus is all we need; indeed, the world needs Jesus.

So how can we seek Jesus in the Lazarus story? I mean really seek him, to gain wisdom and understanding from him. Let us take a look. On the day Lazarus became ill. This was actually good news for his family. Why? Because Jesus was near. He was a family friend, a great healer and only two miles away. All would be well. Jesus was sent for and Lazarus' sisters, Mary and Martha, began caring for him. The next day Lazarus was dead.

Jesus had been going about his business doing God's work, healing the sick and delivering miracles. Yet when the news about Lazarus reached Jesus, even though he was so close, he did not leave immediately. He was needed where he was. Lazarus died some days after Jesus got the news of his illness, but Jesus could not get to him before it was too late. It took four days before Jesus told his disciples that Lazarus was dead, and it was time to go to him. Not to mourn him, as would be expected, but to wake him up! After four days in the grave, Jesus was going to Lazarus in order to bring glory to God his father, displaying the full power of God in him through the astonishing miracle to come.

Of course, no one could have imagined what Jesus was planning to do. Mary did not even come out to meet him with her sister Martha! There was a lot of grumbling and complaining about Jesus' tardiness, how although he loved Lazarus, he did not come when he could have saved his life. So why come now? Both Martha and Mary challenged Jesus with this question, and his answer was to be the headline news everyone was waiting to hear – even if they did not yet know it. '25 Jesus said to her, "I am the resurrection and the life. The one who believes in me will live, even though they die; 26 and whoever lives by believing in me will never die."'

John 10:10 tells us Jesus came to give us life, and life in abundance. Just to exist is not enough for God's children; he planned abundant life for us. So when Jesus is asked how Lazarus could be brought back, given he had been in his tomb for four days and would have an odour, we must know our God would not raise him with anything less than the intention of abundant life for him going forward. Now is that not another great headline? Lazarus will live and live abundantly.

If at the beginning of this chapter, you were discouraged by all the talk of bad news headlines, just think of the good news of Lazarus brought to us in John 11, and the good news of abundant life brought to us in John 10. Everything else would get pushed onto the back pages as the news broke of our Lord declaring to the world 'I am the resurrection'. All that we have to do, remember, is seek and we shall find. We can live in peace and goodness if we truly want it. If we do not, that is up to us, but I firmly believe there is no other way. The way of Jesus is the only way to live. Whatever the bad news headlines, however depressing everything seems, we all can be brought back to abundant life again, just as Lazarus was. However bad things get, our worst experiences need not be the end.

Prayer

Thank you, Heavenly Father, for sending us your son Jesus Christ and all his headline-grabbing miracles. Our Lord Jesus Christ who was, still is and always will be. Thank you for the indescribable gift of his holy presence in our lives, and the record of his deeds we can learn from.

Amen.

53

GRAVE CLOTHES

Paul tells us in Romans 9:21 that we are all part of the same clay, but God takes each lump and makes it into something special, different types of vessels to be used as he sees fit. When he sees the state we get ourselves into, sometimes he must weep! Some of us get ourselves in a terrible mess after he has cleaned us off in his precious blood. Yet because of whom he is, he will clean us off, again and again, enabling us to shine as bright as snow. God does not turn his back on us, in spite of our own undoing. He has mercy on us and allows us to start afresh.

In Chapter 52, I talked about Lazarus in his grave clothes. Jesus called him from the grave, but he still had his grave clothes on. When our Lord Jesus sees us in our grave clothes, lying motionless or wallowing in our sinful state, shameless and disgraced, wrapped up in whatever the world has wrapped us in, his heart is broken. Jesus told Lazarus to take off his grave clothes, and he tells us to do the same. We do not need them anymore once we are restored by him.

Jesus once met a man described as a 'rich young ruler' (Mark 10:17-27). He asked Jesus what to do to get eternal life. Yet he was already walking around in grave clothes as his worldly wealth and concerns were wrapped around him. The Bible tells us he walked away from our Lord when he answered that the rich man should sell all he had, give it to the poor and follow him. That was just too much for him to do. However, we are also told Jesus still loved him. Even if we are restricted by our grave clothes we are still loved.

I heard a sermon from Rick Warren on Premier Radio, where he said a divided church cannot stand, and if we cannot stand, we must fall. In John 17, the Lord prays that we should live together in unity, that we may be one as he and the father are one. So, I believe in these days of sadness the Lord is saying to us, the body of Christ, we need to help each other to take off our grave clothes. Step away from our worldly concerns. With them weighing us down and restricting us, we are living without unity in the body of Christ. We can't just sit at home without anyone looking after the flock. Let us as God's children step out of our own grave clothes and do the work we have been called to do.

Reflection

What are your grave clothes today? Do you have a tomb you need to come out of? We have become so fearful through the pandemic that we risk burying ourselves. God is calling us to stop being so fearful and continue the work he has given us. In spite of the fears of the world, we need to open up the church doors, be with our fellow Christians and worry God with our prayers today.

54

GOD'S GIFT OF MERCY, GRACE & FORGIVENESS (LUKE 5)

Let's talk about mercy, grace and forgiveness. I do not think any of us were born merciful. No, we were we not always merciful people, even if we were given the name Mercy when we were born! Mercy is God's gift to us and can be given in grace. We do not deserve it. We cannot earn it. We must first know this before we can truly accept it. I learned this some time ago, but only understood it quite recently. The Holy Spirit spoke to me about it and the whole idea of mercy began to make more sense to me. Alongside this, I realised we are not naturally forgiving people either. Even we who are born again still find forgiveness hard, it does not come easy. So how can we become more aware of these gifts and their fruits?

There are three passages of scripture we can look at to help us with these three gifts from God. These are the Parable of The Good Samaritan, (Luke 10:25-37), the Parable of The Unmerciful Servant (Matthew 18:21-35) and the prayer the Lord teaches us in Matthew 6:12. So let us explore them a little, taking forgiveness first, although we will see how all three intertwine.

If we have a forgiving spirit, it is because of grace. God has changed our hearts so we can be merciful and make us able to forgive. Forgiveness is not a light thing. Sometimes we have to work at it. So if we have got that forgiving spirit, it is because we have first received grace from God. That enables us to forgive others in spite of who we are. Our Lord Jesus told us if we cannot forgive each other, and truly forgive from the heart, then our heavenly father will not forgive us. We've obtained mercy, so we must be willing to show mercy and we can forgive.

Now if we look at mercy, we might understand better why it is enabling us. The Good Samaritan is a clear example of one full of mercy. In the parable, he takes pity on the man attacked by robbers and takes him somewhere to recover, covering all his bills. This is made all the more extraordinary by the fact he is of a different, and opposing, culture to the wounded man. Micah 6:8 tells us what God desires from us as his children, to act justly and show mercy. Isaiah 58 also tells us what God desires from us. The unmerciful servant from Jesus' parable in Matthew 18 was punished by God because he would not show mercy to his fellow man, and who can stand the wrath of God? Let us take heed.

And now back to grace. Grace has been given to all of us, so we are able to do all these things God demands of us. It has been given, so we receive it and let it flow out of our lives. When we fall short of all that we are given to do, we must turn to the Lord and ask for more of his grace in our lives. He is always willing to help, as he knows our weaknesses. Our strength will forever be in him, and his gifts of grace, mercy and forgiveness.

Prayer

Oh, loving Heavenly Father. Who is like you? There is none besides you who would put up security for one like me. You have put all my yesterdays behind me in spite of my deeds and have brought me into your own future through forgiveness by your grace and mercy. Father God, I thank you for the work done on the cross for me. I acknowledge, O Lord, that it's because of love for the children of man that you have sacrificed all for my sins. Praise, glory and honour belong to you. Thank You, Lord.

Amen.

55

ZACCHAEUS' TESTIMONY
(LUKE 19:1-10)

L uke began this chapter by telling us of a tax collector whom Jesus came to save. His name was Zacchaeus. He was the chief collector of taxes in Jericho and was very wealthy This is a very familiar story to Bible readers and is often told in Sunday schools. I even learned about it in Junior school. It goes like this.

Zacchaeus was a very short man who, having heard about Jesus of Nazareth, wanted to see him. But as I wrote about in Chapter 47, Jesus had an entourage travelling about with him; not only his disciples but there was always a crowd of people following him. Zacchaeus knew it would be difficult to see Jesus past the crowds, so he thought of something creative. Where there is a will there is a way! So Zacchaeus found a way forward through the crowd, got ahead of it and climbed up a sycamore tree. As Jesus was coming near the tree, Zacchaeus thought he would see him, and had hoped something might change for the better in his life.

The true story of Zacchaeus is about someone opening themselves up to a life-changing situation. When someone accepts the Lord Jesus in their lives as their Lord and Saviour, amazing change can happen. It also tells us of a person who may be rich in wealth but poor in the wisdom of God. Zacchaeus was also lonely with few friends. Almost everybody disliked tax collectors, they had a reputation for taking a little more than they should and keeping it for themselves. We all have to pay taxes but we all would like the taxman to be fair. I know I resent paying taxes, especially council tax. What is more, he was collecting for the Romans who were the enemies of the Judeans. Zacchaeus was not in a popular position at all.

So, Zacchaeus was rich yet poor. He was lonely, low and loveless. But God who knew him before he was born, who created him in his mother's womb, noticed his need and came to his rescue. He who put Zacchaeus (and us) together sent his only begotten son to him. Just like in the story of the woman at the well in John 4 (see Chapter 44) Jesus was not passing through randomly but was sent to Jericho on purpose. Yes, the salvation of God was near for Zacchaeus but who was going to tell him? Like the woman in Samaria, those around him would rather see him go to hell and be burned than tell him about Jesus. Zacchaeus may have been able to buy some friends, but they were never going to be genuine. Buying friends might even turn out to be very bad because when your money is gone, they are gone too.

But Zacchaeus must have heard the rumours somehow. He wanted to find out for himself.

Zacchaeus knew he had a problem getting a good view due to his height. So, he made his plan to see Jesus. I believe God was already ploughing the soil of his soul and preparing his heart for the divine intervention to come. God saw his needs and came to his rescue, just as he looks at all our needs, our faults, and rescues us too. Jesus is the friend of the friendless, lover of our souls and come to salvage Zacchaeus (and us) with a promise of a brand-new life. Praise the Lord!

Zacchaeus did not know what was going to happen to him when he came face to face with Jesus. When I started looking for Jesus, I did not know what was going to happen either. I did not even know the scripture that says if we look for him, we will find him (Matthew 7:7). Zacchaeus did not have that promise in his life either. But he took time out from his life to seek out Jesus. He sat up in that Sycamore tree and waited for something to happen. There was no 'can't' in Zacchaeus' life that day, there was only 'must'. He was drawn to the call of God on his life.

How spectacular it must have been when Jesus looked up and saw Zacchaeus there. Jesus said to him, 'Zacchaeus, come down immediately. I must stay at your house today'. He called Zacchaeus by name and saved him by grace. That's what Jesus came into the world for, to save the lost. What next for Zacchaeus? Well, he was instantly changed. When Jesus declared his intention to go to Zacchaeus' house, the crowd protested. Zacchaeus was a sinner. Jesus should not go there! Zacchaeus felt bad, I am sure. So, he said to the crowd 'Look, Lord! Here and now I give half of my possessions to the poor, and if I have cheated anybody out of anything, I will pay back four times the amount.' (Luke 19:8). Quite a change had come into his life and if there is a change, it should be seen.

Reflection

This testimony of Zacchaeus tells all of us who claim to be Christ's followers, that if we accept Christ Jesus in our life, there should be a change in our way of living – and it must be seen. Zacchaeus did not grow taller, but he gained stature. That day, as Jesus told him, salvation came to him.

Praise the Lord for his salvation which comes to us! May the change in our lives be seen throughout our whole lives. That's what Jesus does for us. Praise Him.

Amen.

56

WASHING OF FEET (JOHN 13)

John 13 is perhaps one of the most talked about, or even preached on, passages in the Bible. Indeed, it is full of the last few days of Jesus' earthly life. In it, Jesus washes his disciples' feet, Judas is promoted to the role of betrayer and Peter's denial is predicted. Yet it is the washing of feet which interests me most about this passage.

Jesus told Peter, if I do not wash your feet, you cannot have any part of me (John 13:8). Peter then asked Jesus to wash not only his feet but all of him, to which Jesus answered, 'Those who have had a bath need only to wash their feet; their whole body is clean. And you are clean, though not every one of you.' (John 13:10). In saying this, Jesus showed Judas he knew of the plot against him, which he would reveal later in the chapter.

Jesus went on to tell the disciples that one of them would betray him – even though he had just washed all of their feet. Including those of the one who would betray him. Is that not astounding? What amazing grace. Yet Jesus wants us to follow his example. He directs us in vs. 14-16 to wash each other's feet, as no one person is above another. His call is to love our enemies so much, that even if we know they have ill intent towards us we should love them the same as our dearest friends.

Reflection

There are many verses from across the Bible that connect to this chapter. In John 13, Jesus is reinforcing his entire teaching in these last hours of his ministry.

John 13:34-35 matches his statement in John 15:12, where Jesus tells his disciples to 'Love each other as I have loved you.' Through this radical love, even washing the feet of those we know wish us harm, we will be known as his disciples. To this day, his instruction is true.

Paul tells us in Ephesians 5:1-2, to follow God's example and live a life of love, just as Christ loves us. This confirms John's writing in John 13:1 where he states, 'Having loved his own who were in the world, he loved them to the end.'

In Romans 12:10, Paul begged us to be devoted in love and honour one another above ourselves. This follows the example set by Jesus here in John 13.

I pray that these verses become useful to you as they are to me. May the God of Peace guide and encourage you to follow him, giving you strength and a desire to live a life that is pleasing to him always.

Amen.

57

THE UPSIDE OF SORROWS
(MATTHEW 26:36-45)

While we, as God's people, are all called to rejoice (see Chapter 33), Paul recognises this is not always possible. It is very hard to wear a smile on your face always. The children of Israel were taught to sing a song for the Babylonian soldier. Their reply was, how can we sing the Lord's song while we are in a strange land? (Psalm 137). So, I think it is perfectly reasonable not to go on rejoicing, especially in these very dark days of COVID-19. At the time of writing this chapter, we have had this dreadful disease among us for over two years, and in this country alone we have had over 200,000 people die. How can we rejoice yet?

Yet, we should be able to rejoice as we are supposed to be the happiest people on Earth. We have the greatest thing in heaven and on Earth living inside of us. We have got the Spirit of God in us. Yes. Romans 5:5 tells us that God has poured out his love into our heart, which is giving us the

Spirit. He chose us from the world to be his children. We are the cream of the world before God. John 14:17 tells us that 'the world cannot accept [the Holy Spirit] because it neither sees him nor knows him'. So, we ought to be happy, with the knowledge that we have, but we still cannot go around with a smile on our face all the time. At least I cannot.

People who know me would say I do not smile at all. Not true, I can assure you. I also do belly laugh! But surely if we went around with a grin on our faces all the time, people would think Christians are not quite well. In fact, it is Jesus who calls us to follow him, and we know he was a man of sorrow. I can only find one place in the Gospel where it says Jesus was full of joy (Luke 10:21). He may not always have been sad but certainly most of the time, he was heavy hearted. We know that Jesus attended weddings and dinner parties, which should have been joyous occasions, yet all the time he had to bear the knowledge of what was to come. He was thinking of his death.

I can barely read the end of the four Gospels as they are so sad, but as difficult as they may be, we ought to read them. We should face up to the truth of what our Lord has done to make us the happiest people on Earth. It makes me very sad but the sort of sadness which is good for the soul. Solomon told us in Ecclesiastes 7:3 that sorrow was better than laughter, and Job 42:5 tells us that even though he had previously heard of God, he saw him closest through his grief. I believe God himself grieves when he sees what his creation is up to and how we treated his beautiful son. The Scripture says God turned his face away when Jesus cried out on the cross.

Yes, the upside of sorrow can be good for us. Of course, Jesus' death was sad but come Sunday morning when the very same Jesus raised from the dead grief was turned to joy. There is always a silver cloud behind the darkness, and spring behind winter. Therefore, I encourage you to be strong and bear your grief as best as you can. For weeping may endure for a while, but joy comes in the morning (Psalm 30:5). If we do not allow sorrow to have a place in our life, we will not find the opportunity to grow through it. We are only stifling our sadness or trying to explain it away. We will remain shallow and indifferent. We will never understand ourselves or others as well as we otherwise could.

I believe God can use us more if we allow ourselves to mourn. If we look at some of God's servants in the past, how they suffered, mourned and grieved so badly, it was often in those dark days that God used them best. Think of when Aaron the high priest lost two sons at the same time. God told him not to mourn (Leviticus 10:1-3), yet through his silent grief, he was able to find a way to make things right with Moses (Leviticus 10:19-20). Was Abraham happy when God told him to sacrifice his son (Genesis 22:1-18)? No. What about David when he lost his first son with Bathsheba (2 Samuel 12:18)? Paul had to live with a thorn in his flesh (2 Corinthians 12:7). Bad things do happen to good people and as we grow through our tragedies, we learn more about God, ourselves and the world around us.

As our Lord's time on Earth was ending Matthew 26:21-30 tells us his heart was full of sorrow and sadness, to the point of his death. He had no time for laughter or rejoicing. Shortly after Peter's confession that Jesus was the Messiah, Jesus began to talk about his death. It was always on his mind. Even the disciples became troubled; the Gospels tell us Jesus talked about the baptism of suffering he had to undergo before he left Earth (Mark 10:38), so of course, those who loved him would become concerned. One of the truest upsides of sorrows is they show that we have loved or have been loved. Now that is something worth rejoicing about.

Prayer

Jesus Christ, a man of sorrows. We know we will always have burdens to bear. Help us to carry them bravely and pray for each other as our sisters and brothers carry theirs. Let us remember, though we may weep for now, joy cometh in the mornings. For some of us relief cannot come soon enough, but like spring must wait for the ending of winter so we too have to wait. So let us hold on to our sorrow with dignity and daily take it to the Lord in prayer.
Amen.

58

LIVING A SURRENDERED LIFE
(LUKE 22:39-42)

A re you living a surrendered life? Do you know the song 'I surrender'? To surrender to God is a demand, not a request. It is not an easy thing to do either. To surrender means giving everything you have and every area of your life to and for the sake of Jesus.

In the Garden of Gethsemane, Jesus our Lord willingly surrendered his life for our sins. He says these words, 'yet not my will, but yours be done.' (Luke 22:42). The tempter was trying to cause him to fall, even at the very end of his ministry, but Jesus still surrendered all. God knows we do not deserve redemption but because he loves us so much, the sons of man, he allows his glorious son to be tempted, tried and even to die for us. Now we can go around singing and saying we surrender.

We know all too well what Jesus surrendered. But what do we surrender? There is a song we sing often in my church called 'Take my life and let it be' which I love to pray too.

It goes, 'Take my life and let it be consecrated all for Thee. Take my moments and my days; let them flow in ceaseless praise.' We go on to sing, 'Take my silver and my gold [our money]; Not a mite would I withhold.'

Yet we know that is not true. We sometimes do not even pay tithes. May God forgive us. Yes, we do all have weaknesses. Of course, we need to yield them to God in prayer. We must be willing to let go of all that we are holding on to and allow God to have his way in our whole life. If we do not let him have his way, we cannot surrender.

We have to let God's will be done in us. He has great plans for us. We can of course say yes, he is our Lord. But how much of our life does he truly have? To be fully surrendered to him we must yield all our heart, soul and body, not just in part but as a whole. Only then can we truly say we have surrendered. Now, that does not mean we will not feel pain and hurt. We will still hurt as other people do. All great men and women have felt pain. They have dealt with bad news as well. They have coped with losses, sometimes not even allowed to cry. God told some of them not to cry or mourn. Some things we just have to bear. Yet in our state of surrender, we know we do not need to bear them on our own.

A life that is surrendered to God is a life that is willing to bend to the will of God. I'm not talking about at the time when we got saved. No, I'm talking about a life that is willing to declare that God sent his glorious Son to die for the sins of Adam's fall from grace. Not just once, but every single day. Jesus deserves nothing less, for his path to our salvation was not easy. He knew all about death on a cross, it was a common method of execution by the Romans. But our Lord surrendered to his father's will anyway. If he can do that, then do not say we cannot do what is asked of us. Yes, we can! God has given us all we need to help, the Holy Spirit will always be with us and whatever storm we are going to go through, Jesus will be in our boat to calm it.

Reflection

It is never easy to surrender all to God, even though we sing and pray the words. It is not easy, but it is the only way we can allow God to have his way with our life. It is not a matter of saying we are not perfect; God wants us to be perfect. He gave us his son's blood and the Spirit. He is at our beck and call, always. All we need to do is allow ourselves to think about it and completely give ourselves to God. Jesus went to his father at Gethsemane for his surrender and we must go to Jesus for our surrender. He will help us with this, I know. Say to him this prayer:

'I surrender. All that I think I have is yours. Take it and seal it for your courts above. All to you I freely give.'

Amen.

59

THE TRIAL OF OUR LORD
(LUKE 23:1-12)

Pilate and Herod, two people central to the trial and crucifixion of Jesus, were enemies before they come together on that fateful day. Encouraged by the evil one they were of one accord (Luke 23:12). Although they tried to find our Lord guilty of crimes, they could not, as he was perfect and sinless. Isaiah the prophet foretold hundreds of years before that when the Messiah came, he would be spotless using these words, 'He will not cry out or raise His voice, nor make His voice heard in the streets. A bruised reed He will not break' (Isaiah 42:2-3).

As I was reflecting on Jesus' path to the cross and remembering his words to the weeping women from Luke 23:28 (see Chapter 33) I began to think of the massacre in Myanmar. I can see Jesus' words have been fulfilled there. Pictures of Yemen, child kidnap and torture, terrorists in Africa and many years of war in Syria and Sudan all come to my mind. I remember the words of Jesus that he spoke to the women that if men can do this to him in good times, what will they do in times of hardship? We know how the hearts of men are so wicked and times are getting worse. Our Lord Jesus' words are being fulfilled every day before our very eyes.

Mankind puts our trust in science to improve our situation and not in the Creator who made all things. The one who created science in the first place! Luke himself was a scientist, a medic. Yet he believed in the mystery of Christ so much that he recorded it for the world as the greatest story ever told. Sometimes I think this story also shows us how awful and cruel human beings are. We are the worst of God's creations. Yet he loved us so much he gave us his only begotten Son to die for us. The world was not saved through science, but love.

Reflection

Doxology

33 Oh, the depth of the riches of the wisdom and knowledge of God!
How unsearchable his judgments, and his paths beyond tracing out!
34 "Who has known the mind of the Lord? Or who has been his counsellor?"
35 "Who has ever given to God, that God should repay them?"
36 For from him and through him and for him are all things. To him be the glory forever!
Amen.

(Romans 11:33-36)

60

TOO SOON, TOO SOON O LORD

Too soon. Too soon, O Lord Jesus, you have left the earth. You came down to earth in human form as the babe Jesus, yet your life was to be a short one. You were only 33 years of age when you left this earth, having only shared with us three years of your glorious and wonderful teachings. Too soon, O Lord. Too soon.

Yet, O Lord, you have filled the earth with your righteous and holy deeds and wonders. How wonderful and marvellous you are! Yes, we can joyfully sing 'How Great Thou Art.' As Luke writes, 'you only just began' (Acts 1:1). You only just began to do and to teach until the day you were taken up to heaven. You only just began to work all these miraculous signs and wonders. No one could truly take your life away, yet only three and a half years of your earthly ministry were visible to mortal man.

I would say that I miss you, Lord Jesus, but I know you are here, continuing your unfinished work in our daily lives. Oh, how glorious it is to know this! Not to me only, but to everyone who accepts your teaching. When we know your awesome presence is with us, we have no need to miss you.

Prayer

Praise and thanks to the Triune God, Father, Son and Holy Spirit, for your ever presence.

I just want to say I love you, Lord, and I will worship and honour your great and awesome name. I would desire my heart to be proud, and my eyes to be haughty as I concern myself with great things of you, my Lord and my King.

Help me to quieten myself like a child, be calm and wait upon you, Jesus. Let me give thanks in the knowledge that you have finished the work your father gave you, as you cried out from the cross 'It is finished.' Praise the Lord.

Therefore my heart is steadfast. Yes, Lord, my heart is steadfast as I sing and make music to you, my Lord. I will awake my soul at dawn and praise you among the nations. I will sing among your peoples, for great is your love reaching up to the highest heaven, and your faithfulness to the ends of the earth.

So be exalted, Oh God. Let your glory be over all the earth.

Amen.

61

CALVARY: DEEPEST PAIN
(LUKE 22)

The deepest of pains must have been felt at the Last Supper when our Lord broke the bread and gave some to the betrayer. The group sharing the meal were Jesus' closest friends, and yet Judas would go on to help those arresting him for 30 pieces of silver. The last chapters of the Gospels are so full of cruelty to our Lord, they are difficult to read. One may say he was God, but we must not forget Jesus was Mary's human son also. Yet, I do believe that betrayal is the worst pain, despite our Lord knowing what was going to happen.

To be betrayed is an awful feeling. I have been betrayed and I do know how it feels. Unlike our Lord Jesus, I bore it for at least twenty years. I let the person know how I felt, but I did not make a big fuss about it. I stayed very careful with that person, especially in the presence of others. Our Lord did not have such a privilege. His betrayal was almost instantaneous. Then they journeyed through the pain of Calvary together, suffering the experience of Jesus' execution in their different ways.

The last woman to be executed in America died only recently, in 2021, yet she was on death row for two years. She must have gone through the agony of Calvary. I also know a 17-year-old young man who knew he was going to prison even though he was not at first locked up for his crime, as he waited two years for his trial. That was painful. He greatly regretted his crime. Yet even though both this woman and this man suffered, they had committed crimes. In the end, it was our Lord who was innocent and suffered anyway.

You and I know this had to happen. It is sometimes said bad things happen to good people. This was one of them. How can we ever understand how our Lord Jesus felt in the last three weeks of his earthly life? He knew he would be reunited with God, his Father, but he had also made friends here on Earth. The separation would be even more painful to go through as he loved them so much, despite Judas' act of betrayal. If it is true that this story is the greatest story ever told, let us think about this in human terms, as well as godly terms, and see what we, as lovers of Jesus, true believers, can receive from Calvary's deepest pain.

Think of the shame and humiliation our Lord felt. He carries it to cover us. He hides our shame. The 17-year-old young man I referred to earlier was one of my sons. He got mixed up with a person who forced him to do things he had never done before. Going to prison was hard for him, but I believe it spared his life. Prison became his safe place.

Jesus hid my shame, as I could not talk about it. He hides my son's pain even now after 25 years. In bearing his wounds, he bears ours too. Our Lord was tortured and whipped, bruised for our iniquity. Yet that was on the day of his death. Just think of the three and a half years living with the knowledge of it! I thank Jesus for his sacrifice and ask God to help me learn from this painful story.

Reflection

Isaiah 42:20 tells me 'You have seen many things, but you pay no attention; your ears are open, but you do not listen.' May God help me to see, hear and understand more about Jesus and his crucified self. For there's more. Thank you Father, Son and Holy Spirit, for hiding my shame and my pain in my distress.

Amen.

62

THE ROAD TO EMMAUS
(LUKE 14:13-32)

The Road to Emmaus is a story about going back to where we were before Christ called us. Going back to before we said 'yes' to God through Christ Jesus. At the beginning of our Christian journey, we were walking closely with the Lord, but for many of us, some way along the road something happened, and our paths drifted apart. But for the grace of God, that could be my experience. I am grateful it is not! So, this story is about the conversations we can have if we are open to them, through which Jesus can reveal himself anew and we can be drawn back into his presence again, where we belong.

We often sing this song in church with the lyric, 'We've decided to follow Jesus, no turning back, no turning back.' But a lot of people do turn back. The children of Israel turned back in their hearts when they were wandering in the wilderness. They began to prefer the thought of servitude with the Egyptians over their walk with God in freedom.

Now I find it very hard to understand how anyone would turn away from God and back to an old, cruel master since every day I experience with Jesus is sweeter than the day before. Yet it does happen. People think the grass is always greener on the other side of the fence and do not look at the beautiful garden they have.

The nation of Israel was called to be a light to the world. But as always happens amongst humans, sin crept in, and the situation went from bad to worse. God kept calling and calling the Israelites to come back to him and follow him. But they kept on refusing (see Samuel 8:6-7 and Isaiah 1:2-3). Now, God is never willing to give anyone up to the devil. But when we do develop a spirit of rebelliousness, put our fingers in our ears and harden our hearts, we can easily end up sinning.

Our Lord Jesus once told his followers The Parable of the Sower (Matthew 13:1-23). In this story, a farmer is sowing seeds (which in the story represent people) on his land. Some fall among the thorns, meaning the world will get hold of those people either by wealth or by lifestyle. The things of the world will choke them, as the thorns would choke the new growth of the seeds. If we turn away from God and towards the things of the world, any new growth we may have will be choked too. But we are fortunate in that the God we worship is patient and kind. Jesus is still calling and waiting for us to come back to him, however long it takes. Do you understand that he is holding out his hand to you as the father holds his arms out to the prodigal son (Luke 15:11-32)?

I tell you, God's love for mankind is beyond limits. Some might think God is a weak God, because of the way he speaks so tenderly to his people at times throughout the Bible. But it is not a weakness. It is pure love. Look at God's anguish in Hosea 11. In verse 8, he asks of the rebellious Israel, 'How can I give you up?' It makes you want to cry, and it saddens my heart that we have treated God so badly when he loves us so deeply. If you read Isaiah 1:1-2 and understand what God says about his people, it is perfectly reasonable to think God is deeply saddened when one falls away and refuses to come back. I just don't know how anyone called to God could stop loving Jesus our Lord, Emmanuel, God with us. His name is so sweet, sweeter than anything you could think of. He is all I want in life.

I think part of our trouble is that we do not want to be accountable to anyone. We enjoy the feeling of being around Jesus, but when the initial excitement fades and we have to put the hard work in, we drift away. We start to go back to where we came from, back to Emmaus. We want to bring the world into the church, mix our two separate lives for the wrong reasons as we become weak and unkind in sin. We become the seed that falls among thorns. Yet thankfully God is gracious. He has prepared a way out for every one of us. Jesus Christ is the way indeed, and he will always welcome us back to his side with tender loving care.

Prayer

Lord God who waits patiently for all who fall astray. I pray for any of us who feel lost, who are at a crossroads or who, at the first sight of any little obstacle we come upon, think of going back to where God called us from in the first place. May God help us all to come to our senses and return back to him in humility and repentance. In spite of all our foolish and prideful ways, take us back and lavish love on us by your grace and mercy, so we will feel the bliss of our walk with you anew. May we be reinstated in full through your compassion and generosity.

Thanks and praise be to our God and Father of our Lord Jesus Christ the way maker.

Amen.

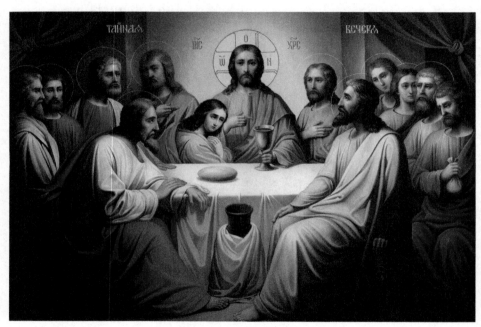

Calvary's deepest pain

63

BROKENNESS CAN PRECEDE
BLESSING (JOHN 21)

To those who are called to be fishers of men. If you do not catch fish, please do not fight it. Do not be disappointed or feel broken. If you see snow and ice that hardens the water and stops you from catching fish, do not give up. Do not begin to point fingers and find someone else to blame for the problems you face. Remember, you could be facing the work of the devil, and if so, you do not fight against flesh and blood but against principalities and powers of darkness. So, take a deep breath, swallow hard and stand firm in the strength God gives you. Keep holding on to the desire to be fishers of men. For even when we are broken and all seems lost, God uses us still.

The Bible is full of people who were broken, at the end of their tether or in a place of isolation when God entered their lives to use them. Through these people, such as Moses, David and Elijah, he revealed his power in remarkable ways. If we truly believe in these stories, we must believe brokenness can produce blessings. I sometimes wonder if we have not come to that place of brokenness of spirit, can we fully be placed into action within God's great plans for us? I can tell you for sure he has great plans for us as his children. Otherwise, there would be no reason for him to call us out of the darkness, our own Egypt, and into his light (see Chapter 8). So, I encourage you, do not be dismayed in your brokenness. It can be for your own good.

Take Simon Peter. Once Jesus had been killed, Simon Peter returned to his fishing boat. He went back to where he was before Christ called him into repentance. He had denied Jesus three times and was ashamed. He was broken. Yet Jesus our Lord came back to life, back to Simon Peter, and reinstated him through his blessing (John 21:15-19). To the end of his days, Simon Peter was called to be a fisher of men despite his brokenness and sin. Even though all may seem broken and lost in the world today, God can still use us in his great plans. How incredible is that?

Prayer

Thanks be to God for your great mercy, you who gives us all a second chance despite our flaws and brokenness. We praise you that you have such great plans for us, which turn our brokenness into blessings. Looking to our Lord Jesus with his love and kindness, his great compassionate heart, we thank you for his example in our lives. He reinstated Simon Peter, and we know he will do the same for us, Lord. Thank you that even in the face of the devil, your strength is enough. Give us more of it each day, so our brokenness can precede blessing in our own lives, and in the lives of others.

Amen.

64

JERUSALEM AWAITS HIM

P aul the Apostle preached and taught repentance to both Jews and Gentiles alike, in a time when this was not yet commonly agreed upon. He instructs all peoples that they should turn to God in repentance and have faith in Christ Jesus, as Jerusalem awaits him. These words and the promise of hope contained within them bring tears to my eyes. Jerusalem awaits Jesus' return still to this day.

Paul asks those to whom he was preaching to pray all sorts of prayers through his letters. He was often going through rough patches in his ministry when he was writing, and it is clear he felt the spiritual weight of what might happen to him in Jerusalem. Remember, Paul had once persecuted the followers of Christ for the Jewish establishment there, before he had been converted to Christ's path himself on the road to Damascus. So, he asked for prayers, modelling his requests on those Jesus made in his days on Earth. Paul said we must pray, not for him alone, but for brothers and sisters who may also be going through difficult times on their pilgrim journeys. Paul, through the Holy Spirit, knew what difficulties awaited him in Jerusalem, just as Jesus had known. I can feel it as I am writing this chapter, the movement of the Holy Spirit compelling Jesus our Lord to set his face Jerusalem, despite the fate he would meet there. He did not flinch, my brothers and sisters. He met his fate well. For he knew it was not the end, and he would rise again.

I invite you now to put yourself in the place of one awaiting trial as our Lord Jesus did. Imagine knowing you are going to go to prison as you leave home to go before the judges. As I write this, I remember the face of Derek Chauvin who murdered George Floyd in America. I could not have felt sorrier for George Floyd, whose death highlighted the Black Lives Matter movement globally. He did not know he was going to die as he left his house that day. If we were to face our day of judgement today, would our hearts be pure? Would we pass judgement and find ourselves a place in heaven?

There is a new song being sung by a songwriter called Zach Williams which says, 'I am no longer a slave to sin. I am now a child of God.' I give thanks and praise to the Almighty God for his great wisdom, strength and love for mortal man which allowed his son to go through hell on Earth for our sake. Wretches like us can now declare we are children of God in churches up and down the land. Hallelujah! Yet we know this is not all the good news, because Jerusalem awaits Jesus still. We know he will return. Because we are no longer slaves to sin through his death on the cross, even if our sins were as grievous as persecuting fellow men, as Paul's were, we get our invitation to the new Jerusalem when Jesus comes back. Is that not incredible?

Prayer

Lord Jesus, I thank you that in my weakness, I know I can depend on you. You are my strength, my portion, my high tower. Praise you, O Lord, for all your goodness. You make me lie down in green pastures and refresh my soul with deep spiritual rest. Praise and glory to you, O mighty God.

As we await the return of your son Jesus to Jerusalem, I thank you for giving me the honour of becoming your child. I know it's not because I'm worthy to be blessed, but through blessing me and others like me, O Lord, your name may be renowned throughout the Earth. Thank you for all you have done for us, as we await the new Jerusalem.

Amen.

Part Three

LIVING AS A CHURCH

65

A PRAYER FOR THANKSGIVING

My heart is steadfast, O Lord, my God. So I will sing and make music to you. Awake, my soul, Awake! Awake with harp and lyre. I will awake the dawn and I will praise you, Lord among the nations. I will sing among the peoples, for great is your love reaching up to the heavens, and your faithfulness to the skies. Be exalted, O my God, far above the heavens. Let your glory be over all the earth.

Holy Father, there is none like you. I just want to worship and adore you. We know we fail most of the time, yet you catch us with love when we do. It's good to know all that you have given us to know about you in the Bible, so we can trust you, God who is great, merciful, gracious, full of compassion and love. You look upon us with adoration and show mercy on us. We are so thankful that you are so patient with us. Thank you, Lord.

Thank you for being the compassionate God who is still calling us to repentance. We are so blessed that your love for mankind goes beyond all bounds. We know that because of your love for us, you sent your only son to die for us. You do not truly treat us as our sin deserved, and we stand in awe of you for your benevolence. You continually hold out your hands towards us as a father to a child, calling to us despite our unwillingness to return to you. O merciful Father, you are so wonderful, so mighty in power and awesome in judgement.

I love you Father, Son and Holy Spirit, and commit my life to you completely. Even though I am weak and frail, I know, O Lord, that you can still use even me, in spite of all my faults. That's who you are. I know you have a purpose for my life. Use me where you desire. Use me here in this street where I live to share your love with my neighbours Help my light to shine so that others may see you in me. Let the life I live speak to your glory. I pray this not for my sake Lord, but for yours.

I pray for the church that bears your name, dear Lord. I pray that you will indeed send a revival to our land. Revive your church in Britain again, I pray. Pour on us a Pentecostal shower of your Holy Spirit. Stir up your children to receive your mighty gifts. Review our worthiness, increase our faith and all the other gifts you give us, your children.

Instil in us the knowledge of your holy presence that is with us always. I ask you to hear this, my prayer, and grant all that is favourable to you. In Christ Jesus' name, I pray.

Amen.

66

CORPORATE WORSHIP

Corporate worship is very important for more than one reason. People need other people, and God's desire is the fellowship of believers. The gathering of God's people is called the assembly of the congregation, meaning more than one person. It is true that when we are on our own, we must worship God; we cannot always be together as an assembly or congregation. But all throughout the Bible God tells us to congregate and worship him.

God has always given clear instructions about how he is to be worshipped. In Deuteronomy 12:4-6, Moses was instructed to tell the Israelites not to worship the Lord in any old place they thought they should go, but to gather at the place the Lord allowed his Spirit to dwell. They and their families should go and take their tithes and offerings, sharing in the act of worship as a community together. Paul talked about how to worship God, although I am not sure how women of today will accept the strict dress code of 1 Corinthians 11! Paul went on to tell us about communities, which is perhaps the key to his earlier instructions. We should come to worship dressed in a manner which respects the community we share in. I think that will be more satisfactory to the women of today.

How we are within our bodies when we come to worship matters too, not just our outward appearance. James 4:8 tells us to wash our hands and purify our hearts when we come to hear God, for cleanliness is important to him. Chronicles 16:32-End shows us how joyful you can feel when God's people worship together. We can see good examples of this in David's exuberant Psalms, most notably Psalm 29 and Psalm 100. In contrast, Solomon tells us in Ecclesiastes 5:1 to come close and listen to the words of God. He doesn't mean to rush in, but to come in slowly, sit down gently and listen carefully. We are in the presence of God Almighty, so bow down in reverence before him. bend the heart and pay attention.

When we are in corporate worship with others, this continues as the pastor speaks. The way we listen to them is worship too, we must still be respectful of God and the message he has given the pastor to preach. Take notes if you wish, but your whole being should be observing what you are listening to. If you agree with what you hear, say amen. If you are not satisfied with what you hear, go home and read your Bible more. Pray while you do so and ask the Lord to open your mind so you can further understand what you are reading. Take notes again, as you may still go over the same information. Invite the Holy Spirit to intercede for you, but don't stop until you are satisfied. When content with what you have learned and understood, give thanks and praise to the Lord. For in him all things are revealed. Then we can go back into corporate worship confident our hearts are clean and our minds are settled, ready to be with God and our fellowship once more.

Prayer

More and more, Lord Jesus, we desire to walk in the light of your way. But we know we cannot do it in our own strength. Lord, please help us. Please open our eyes and the windows of our minds so our spirits are fully ready to embrace your teaching. Increase your Holy Spirit in us, dear Lord Jesus, filling us with wisdom and the desire to worship you. Increase in us the spirit of discernment, so we will be able to see, hear and understand your teachings. These things we ask in your precious name, Lord Jesus.

Amen.

67

DON'T JUST SIT THERE!
(ACTS 1:20-26)

After the death of our Lord Jesus Christ, it became quite clear that a replacement would have to be found for Judas. So, the disciples made a decision to select someone who knew Jesus and walked in his company. They prepared two men and began to pray. Notice they placed prayer as the most important part of the process. After they prayed, the disciples cast lots which fell on Matthias, and he was selected. Again, notice they did not sit down and wait for God to answer their prayer. They cast their lots, which tells me although we pray first, we must also take action.

This couplet of prayer and action is echoed in Samuel 10:6-7, when Samuel anointed Saul to be the first king of Israel. Following God's blessing, Saul asked Samuel what was next for him. Whatever your hand turns to, God will be with you, came the reply. We have got the Holy Spirit to guide and lead us. We should do whatever our hands find to do that is good and right. God will guide and lead us to the good and right path. Take Esther when she learned that the King's advisors were plotting to eliminate the Jews. She asked her uncle and mentor Mordecai what to do, and after taking advice from him she spent time fasting and praying to God. Through a combination of prayer and action she was able to approach the King, a very brave act, reveal the truth and save the Jewish nation. Daniel is another character in the Bible who combined prayer and action throughout his life to bring glory to God. These are just a few of the biblical people of God who combined prayers for help with decisive action to further the works of the Lord.

Jesus did not promise to run our lives for us. No. He said he would be with us in all things, and in whatever situation we find ourselves in. Jesus will always be by our side to help us, but we must not just sit there waiting for him to do something. We must do something ourselves while we wait for a response from God our Father. Even when great wars are being fought or great disasters are being tackled, we must take action while we pray. Yes, God goes out with the army and works with the healers, coming alongside man in all kinds of trials and tribulations.

We may think that God avoids war, but sometimes he directs it. For example, God told David to go after his enemy the Amalekites after they attacked his stronghold at Ziklag, burned it to the ground and took the women of the camp captive (1 Samuel 30). God told David he could pursue and overtake the Amalekites to rescue the lost families. God had allowed the enemy to burn down the Ziklag. He could have stopped them, but he did not. Sometimes he guides our actions to reveal his purposes, and in this instance, he wanted to bless David with a great victory. When the Israelites were attacked while they were in the wilderness, Moses did not leave their salvation to God through prayer only. Moses told Joshua to be ready to fight, and God was with him in the battle (Exodus 17:8-16). There are times when it is right and just to fight for God's purposes to be fulfilled.

The most important thing to remember is we must go to God first with whatever our problems may be. We absolutely must pray, but we must also do something along with our prayer. For example, there are a lot of leaders and pastors who are shepherding God's people and telling their church members not to take the COVID-19 vaccine. These leaders believe that if they pray, God will help them without taking the vaccine. Big mistake. God has provided this vaccine as help! We prayed and asked God for help, and God provided it in the form of the vaccine, yet these leaders are refusing it and instructing their people not to take it. They don't see this as God's answer to all those prayers.

We must also discern with the Holy Spirit to make sure God is leading our thoughts, otherwise, we could be acting on our own ideas and not God's instruction. Read the Bible with a discerning spirit also; if your discerning spirit is low, ask the Lord to increase it. Make arrangements with like-minded people to get together and pray – that in itself is doing something. Pray for people in leadership and power. Pray for lawyers, doctors, nurses, presidents, prime ministers and people who are in authority. Pray for wisdom for ourselves and others who lead us. In all things, take action. Then God can work in and through all things.

Reflection

Let us open our eyes and see the awesome works God is still doing, by himself and also through the life of his wonderful son Jesus Christ. If we invite God into our lives through prayer and trust in him with our actions, we can accomplish so much. I encourage you to ask of God in the name of Jesus, and you shall receive. Ask for the cleansing of your heart so that you can truly live a life of worship and respect for your Lord and Saviour. In his name, all things are possible, if you do not just sit there and get on with doing his work!

68

A SECOND CHANCE (ROMANS 6)

In Romans 6:1, Paul asked the question, 'What shall we say, then? Shall we go on sinning so that grace may increase?' By no means. God sent his son so we would not die to sin; how can we live in it any longer? We know that where sin abounds, grace increases all the more (Romans 5:20). So, do we go on sinning knowing that there is grace to cover us? The answer is no. We are those who died to sin – yes, died. That is our past tense. Our first life has gone, finished. That was it, past. We buried it in our watery baptism. Our first chance has gone, and we are living in our second chance. When we committed to being baptised in acknowledgement of our new life in Christ Jesus, we put to death that life of sin and we cannot live in it anymore since it is dead and gone. Then our second chance came into force and God our Father made our baptismal covenant with us, washing away our old selves and raising us washed clean into a new life. Just as he did with Christ Jesus, our Lord.

So now we have got our second chance, let us not blow it.

Peter 3:21, tells us our baptism symbolises the resurrection of our Lord Jesus from the dead. Therefore, once we are baptised we have a responsibility to live out the change in our lives, demonstrating how we have been washed clean and born again into new life. Romans 6:12, says 'Therefore do not let sin reign in your mortal body so that you obey its evil desires.' This goes back to obeying the desire of the flesh rather than what God has set in our hearts. We know our God is a God of a million chances. But we must not go on deliberately sinning, since we are already dead to sin and have made the commitment to live that way.

The author of Hebrews 6:6 explains it as we are only crucifying Jesus again each time we sin, may God forbid. Even though I know God will forgive me, I feel ashamed when I do the same thing over and over again when I know it displeases him. I feel ashamed and I have to go back to God again to seek forgiveness. I must do it since I cannot have any peace if I do not put things right with him. I would feel so disgusted with myself. So, I go to God quickly, repent and receive my forgiveness.

To sum up what I am saying. Even though we get a second chance and so on and so forth, we should not take liberties with the sacrifice of God's son. In Luke 20:17, the Gospel writer tells his friend Theopolis about a reference from Psalm 118:22, in which the psalmist rejoices that the stone the builders rejected has become the cornerstone. Jesus had told his followers a parable before revealing that he himself was the cornerstone foretold. He was to be rejected, yet he had come to be the cornerstone of our new lives. So, we should not take liberty with him since he is the one who takes the weight of everything we build in our new lives. Paul put it this way; we should offer ourselves as people who have been brought back from death to life. Let us take that chance with every breath we breathe. If we do this with sincerity, our God the Father of our Lord Jesus Christ will help us at every step of the way.

Prayer

Heavenly Father, I thank you for the second chances you gave. I owe a deep debt of gratitude to them. I know, Lord, it is your nature of grace which causes you to give us these second chances, time and time again. I am so happy and accepting of them.

I praise you, My God, and I rejoice from deep within my soul. I am humbled by the knowledge of your unfailing love, and I will continue to give you the praise and honour that is due to you alone. Thank you for the knowledge that you will help me each time I stumble or fall. Thank you, O most holy one, for every chance you continue to give. Thanks be to God and Father of our Lord Jesus Christ for this wonderful gift of salvation.

Amen.

69

SLAVES TO RIGHTEOUSNESS

2 Hear me, you heavens! Listen, earth!
For the Lord has spoken:
'I reared children and brought them up,
but they have rebelled against me.
3 The ox knows its master,
the donkey its owner's manger,
but Israel does not know,
my people do not understand.'

(Isaiah 1:2-3)

This makes me so sad, for I know it's true. I believe we have lost our way of acknowledging God the Almighty. We are so rebellious against our Maker. We are so disrespectful towards him, so disobedient and rude, so arrogant and boastful. We have no respect. Is it any wonder God speaks to us like that in verse three?

Our Lord Jesus was not always used to encountering people who respected his authority. Luke 7:1-9 tells of the man from Capernaum who counted himself unworthy of asking Jesus into his home to heal someone else. He appropriately acknowledged Jesus, showing him the respect that was due to him and his authority. Jesus was surprised and said these words: 'I tell you, I have not found such great faith even in Israel.' Why? Because he came on his own and they did not receive him.

Jesus is our Lord and Saviour. He deserves to be honoured, worshipped and adored. He came to change things for us; if and when we meet him, and acknowledge him for who he is, he will change our lives. The thing is, we do not hold him in great esteem. Isaiah the prophet did tell us in chapter 53 that we do not esteem him. Yet he has taken up our infirmities and carried our sorrows. He was smitten by the Father for our sake.

I mentioned earlier about our rebelliousness; rebellion is when someone knows they are doing wrong yet continues to do it. Paul tells us in Romans 1:1-24 that the wrath of God is being revealed against the godlessness of people who suppress the truth by their wickedness. Verse 19-21 says:

since what may be known about God is plain to them, because God has made it plain to them. For since the creation of the world God's invisible qualities—his eternal power and divine nature—have been clearly seen, being understood from what has been made, so that people are without excuse.

For although they knew God, they neither glorified him as

God nor gave thanks to him, but their thinking became futile,
and their foolish hearts were darkened.

So, God gave them over to their depraved behaviour, filled
with the desire for immorality and a lack of respect in spite
of what he had done for them. If we accept who we are, and
who God is, through his saving grace, we will surely become,
or desire to be, slaves to righteousness. So let us consider the
marvellous works of the Lord and give him the praise he
so rightly deserves while considering how we show him the
respect he is due.

Prayer

Let us pray. Lord, grant us wisdom. Please, Lord,
increase the spirit of discernment. Open the
windows of our minds so that we may see, hear and
understand what you are doing in our lives, our
communities, our churches, our cities and villages
and in parliaments all over the world. So, we may
really esteem you more, that all the people praise
you. Father, Son, and Holy Spirit.
   Amen.

70

THE WORKING OF
THE HOLY SPIRIT

Before Jesus our Lord returned to heaven, he gave his disciples the instruction not to leave Jerusalem but to wait for a gift. 'For John baptised with water, but in a few days you will be baptised with the Holy Spirit' (Acts 1:5). Jesus told the disciples they would receive power from on high, unlimited power. This power would be enough to give them the courage and authority to continue God's work on Earth. Shortly after this, after Jesus had ascended into heaven, the confused and frightened disciples did receive that which they had been promised. It came to them on a day which is now called Pentecost.

The Feast of Pentecost marks the day when the Holy Spirit came in the fullness of power to the twelve disciples and all who were hiding together following Jesus' ascension, in the upper room they had used for the Last Supper. Now it is my belief at that time Simon Peter did already possess the Holy Spirit. Why? I believe Simon Peter had the Spirit of discernment within him, for he was able to respond with the knowledge of who Jesus truly was when Jesus asked, 'Who do you say I am?' (Matthew 16:15-16). Simon Peter was the one to recognise that Jesus was the Christ, the Messiah. It was also Simon Peter who raised the suggestion that the group needed someone to replace Judas the Betrayer as a twelfth disciple. We could say these are examples of spontaneous things that just happened, but I would say these are actually examples of the Holy Spirit already at work in Simon Peter.

Luke 9:1 tells us Jesus sent the disciples out with all his power and authority, to drive out demons and to cure diseases. Now, where did that power come from if not the Holy Spirit? That was before the Pentecostal experience. Now you and I know no one can do the things that the disciples did when our Lord sent them out two by two without the power of the Holy Spirit. None of us can do such things by our own strength. It is only through God's mighty spirit that we have the power. I believe that sometimes God gives us a one-off blessing to do miraculous works, above and beyond the standard gifts we are given for our daily lives. In Exodus 31:1-6, God told Moses he had filled Bezalel and Oholiab with the Holy Spirit for a particular purpose, therefore setting a precedent, and I think this is what happened to the disciples in this Bible passage.

Now since the day of Pentecost, everyone who has accepted and received Jesus into their lives has been blessed with the presence of the Holy Spirit in their hearts. The

Holy Spirit is called by many names throughout the Bible, such as the comforter, the Spirit of truth, the advocate and the counsellor (John 14). All of these qualities are the same Spirit. It works in many ways as Luke tells us when writing Acts 2. On that day of Pentecost, it came in power like a mighty rushing wind and it filled the room the disciples were in with a glow like tongues of fire. If you have ever felt the Holy Spirit move in you it can feel like a fire has shot up in your very core, or at times it might feel like a bucket of cold water has been poured out on you. It really does come in power, in that it releases some sort of power in you. What an incredible feeling it is, like no other.

The coming of the Holy Spirit also reveals the truth to you. It is often said in the Bible it will reveal, or testify to, God's truth. You cannot hide from the Holy Spirit. It often surprises you and catches you out when you think you are being crafty. On the other hand, the Holy Spirit encourages you when you are discouraged and lifts you up when you are feeling weak. There is no better comfort for you in times of distress. Sometimes the Holy Spirit will move with great power, but other times you may feel it as a strong, quiet presence settling with you as you grieve, reassuring you as you are anxious and staying with you as you struggle to sleep when you are weary. However you need it to be, it will be, even if that is quiet solace rather than extraordinary power.

Simon Peter and the other disciples did have extraordinary power when the Holy Spirit came upon them.

They had increased courage and their stammering tongues were loosened. The Holy Spirit made them feel brave and encouraged Simon Peter especially to be bold and strong, even though his weakness and denial had taken place only a short while before. He and his friends had denied Jesus, ran away and hidden in fear, but in spite of all we may or may not have done God is able to use us anyway. Paul writes that it is through the strength which God has given, and his grace, I am who I am (1 Corinthians 15:10), and this is the same for all of us. We can all declare those words as God is fair, just and willing to give his children his gifts. We are no different from all who have gone before or who will come after. We have received the Holy Spirit, but we must recognise it in our lives and go in the strength of our God-given power. He will authorise, direct, guide and develop each and every one of us, allowing the manifestation of its power in us.

Jesus told us if we, who are mere men know how to treat our children, how do you think our Heavenly Father will treat us? Would he withhold the Holy Spirit if we asked for it? So, in spite of how we feel about anything, our worthiness or our confidence in God, we should always ask, seek and knock at God's door in the hope of receiving the infilling of the Holy Spirit. God will hear, understand and respond. Remember, the Holy Spirit is God's gift to his children after Jesus' death, to continue his work on this Earth. There may be a wait, as the disciples were instructed to wait in

Jerusalem, but your patience will be rewarded. A thousand days in his sight is just like an evening gone in God's time! So do please pray and wait; you will receive power from on high.

Prayer

Our loving Heavenly Father. I am so thankful to know of you and desire to know more of you. Thank you for letting me see into your heart and know you answer prayer. You answer these prayers I have written in this book and you answer the prayers that lie deep in our hearts. You›re widening the narrowness of my heart so I can experience more and more of you. You are increasingly revealing your Holy Spirit in me. I am so blessed by your Holy Spirit and the gifts that you have given me, Lord. Thank you so much.

Amen.

71

FOR NO MATTER HOW MANY PROMISES GOD HAS MADE, THEY ARE 'YES' IN CHRIST. (2ND CORINTHIANS 1:20)

Let us take a good look at this verse. From Genesis to Revelation, God tells us who he is to us human beings. If only we would let ourselves come to a deeper understanding of his loving kindness shown to us by his great compassion and mercy. If only we would accept his parenthood. If only we would acknowledge him, and the love he wants to give and lavish on us. In this chapter, we will look at some of these promises he told us, times when he was there for us, and remind ourselves of the God who wants to care for us, the children of men.

God proved his faithfulness in all his ways. His great promise to Abraham and Sarah he fulfilled. Even though they waited long after a woman would expect to bear a child, God still delivered and kept his promise with the birth of Isaac. God remembered Lot because of his promise to Abraham when trouble came upon Lot. Although we grieve God time and time again, he still is merciful and compassionate to his children.

Then there is the story of God promising safety to Jacob in Genesis 46:2-4. Hard times came to all the surrounding nations around Jacob, seven years of famine, so God told Jacob to go to Egypt and promised he would go with him. Therefore, Jacob went to Egypt. Now consider that promise fulfilled. Next, in Exodus 3:7-15, we are told God saw the misery of the Israelites and sent Moses and Aaron to rescue them. Another promise was fulfilled.

Even though sometimes more often or not, we test God to the limit, God hasn't turned his back on us. He sent prophets, priests, kings, judges and others to lead and guide his children right up to the coming of Christ Jesus. God has kept his promises in spite of how his children behave, and we do behave badly. He remembers his promises, such as those he made to Naomi, Ruth, Boaz and many more in their poor states. He remembered Elizabeth and Zechariah, John the Baptist's parents, and covered Mary's shame. Then Jesus came along, representing God the Father here on earth, the same God who said to Abraham and Jacob, I will be with you. He still is.

Jesus now tells us he will be with us, just as it were. It's the same today. God has not changed nor will he ever. He is constant. Time and time again, he comes to our rescue. In spite of everything, God is still doing so now in our lives if

IN SPITE OF ... *REFLECTIONS ON FAITH*

we let him. He was, he is and always will be. What a mighty God we have! There is not anything you can do for God to change his mind about his plan for your life. He would change you, or he will change you so that his plan for you can succeed, but his will shall be done. Psalm 138:8 says the Lord will fulfil his purpose in your life, whatever it may be. For those who take refuge in him, his eyes are on you. Praise God. Those who were not told about him will see him, and those who have heard the good news will understand. This is happening right now throughout the world. People everywhere are hearing and understanding and turning to Jesus. Praise the Lord.

Prayer

We will praise you, Lord. We will bow down before you and worship you for you are worthy. We thank and praise, worship and adore you for all you are to us and more. Thank you, Father.
Amen.

72

STAND ON THE PROMISES OF GOD

I t appears that the world is telling us there is nothing sinful anymore. Even our leaders who are supposed to be the shepherds of their flocks are trying to convince us not to take the Bible at face value. This may be the opinion of some, but our brother Paul tells us in 2 Timothy 4:3-4 that the time will come when people will not like some of the sound doctrines and instead will find teachings to suit their own desires. They will gather around in great numbers where teachers speak what they want to hear. They will turn their ears away from the truth and into the noise of the world. Paul writes these things around 2000 years ago, yet they are now being fulfilled in our days.

Do our leaders and preachers even understand or believe what they are preaching from the pulpit? Sometimes I am not sure. But God tells Jeremiah that he knows what they are doing, and that he is watching (Jeremiah 7:11). We are being encouraged not to let anyone mould us into their own ways which may not be those of God. We must stand on what we know is the truth, that we find in our Bibles and that has been grounded by the Holy Spirit in our heart and mind. Do not be complacent or compromise in any part of what we've been taught. Ask the Lord to help us in prayer. For we know our fight is not with flesh and blood but with the powers of darkness.

So let us bring God into whatever our concern may be and rely on the discernment the Holy Spirit bestows upon us. For the Holy Spirit is our promised help, and we stand on the promises of the Lord always.

Prayer

Dearest Lord Jesus, as I write and reflect on staying true to your Word, I seek with my whole heart and mind to stand on your promises. I want to thank you so much for your guidance and the wisdom of Paul, who wrote down words of encouragement to help us on our journey with you. You know that the deceiver does his best to lead us, your children, astray as we seek your face. We thank you Lord for your constant guiding hands upon our life, protecting us from all who wish to do us harm on our journey with you. Praise and thanks be to you, our dearest Lord.

Amen.

73

HIS TEMPTATION AND OURS
(JAMES 1:14)

Until we are born again, the only kind of temptation we can understand is the one mentioned in James 1:14 which states, 'but each person is tempted when they are dragged away by their own evil desire and enticed'. Yet when we are saved, we are granted access to another realm alongside the world around us, where there are temptations like the ones our Lord Jesus had to face in the wilderness. Then we are tempted on a different level entirely. We can never reach that stage until we are truly born again and become like Jesus through baptism, born again through the spirit, the water and the blood of Christ.

Baptism is only an outward sign of commitment to those who witness it. You also have to start living the change that came into your life from Christ our Lord. Remember when salvation came to Zacchaeus, the tax collector's house? See what he did? And I say see, because those who were with him when he received salvation were able to see, the change in him straightaway. He acknowledged his sin, offered to repay and thus repented, showing something had happened. If we want Jesus in our lives, he can indeed form such change in us. Jesus says in John 17:21, 'I am in you and you in me'. Paul prayed for us in Galatians 4:9 that Christ be born in us. Our Lord would not ask for something that is impossible. He is our God, Saviour and friend.

Look at it this way. The devil does not tempt us to make us do wrong things. The devil's object is to make us lose what God puts in us through the reforming of our minds. No, Satan only wants to prevent the fulfilment of God's promises that would otherwise be worked out through Christ Jesus in you. Literally, change your mind about Jesus. That's his plan, that's our temptation, and only the Holy Spirit can detect it. Temptation is a test of possession held within the inner spiritual part of our being. Are we following our own desires, or are we with Jesus?

Jesus remembered with his disciples in Luke 22:28 that they were together during his trials and temptations. He went on to say, 'And I confer on you a kingdom, just as my Father conferred one on me.' (Luke 22:29). Jesus was not arrested yet. Some might say Peter denied him and other apostles ran away. But Jesus wasn't talking about that part of his story. He was talking about the day-to-day walk they all took together when he was bearing insults and all that was thrown at him. That's when we need to stand with our friends, when the knives are turning in their backs, or they are going through the most difficult times. That's when the disciples were there. That's where we ought to be with our friends.

The mode of following Jesus changed from the time Judas betrayed him. As soon as situations got tough, things changed. Many turned back. And as it were with Christ Jesus, so it will be with us. Throughout Jesus' time on earth, temptations were always with him, and with his friends. Remember, Judas was with him as one of the disciples. We know from the Bible those who wanted to follow Jesus really felt his sadness at that time. I felt really sad as I wrote this since I've been in difficult situations with friends leading to sad times for us all.

So, the question is, are we going on with him still, in spite of everything? 'Follow me' he said. Sometimes we may feel like hiding ourselves from some of the things God allows around us, but may it never be. It is him, God, who engineers our circumstances, and whatever they may be, we must face them while continuing to resist temptation. For he who is tempting us is also tempting God. So, I ask, are we going on with Jesus all the way? Our Lord's honour is at stake here in our bodily lives. The way is long and goes until there's no longer a trace of footprints to follow, but only a voice. A still voice saying, 'Follow me.'

Reflection

'Come, follow me,' Jesus said, *'and I will send you out to fish for people.'* (Matthew 4:19). May he help us all.

74

WISDOM (1 CORINTHIANS 1:18)

Proverbs 4 tells us to get wisdom at any cost, but where is wisdom to be found? Job asks this question too in Job 28. Right now I think we live in a time of darkness where wisdom is concerned. Mortals have put an end to physical darkness through the Lord giving us great minds of science and gifted people, who found ways to provide physical light in dark spaces. But we are not necessarily wise still. This is why I use the word 'physical' since I believe as a people we are still in spiritual darkness. Human beings have found everything under the heavens that there is to be found. Yet we cannot find wisdom. We have no idea where understanding dwells. The birds of the air say they haven't got it. The deep won't reveal it. It cannot be bought, not at any price. So where does wisdom come from?

Bearing in mind Solomon was said to be one of the wisest people ever to walk on Earth, let us take a look at what he says about finding wisdom Solomon calls wisdom the most valuable asset a human being can possess (Proverbs

4:13). I believe that until we acknowledge Jesus Christ as Messiah, the very Son of God until we accept his death and resurrection and the truth that he died to save us, we will not find wisdom. To find wisdom is to know Christ Jesus, for he is wisdom, knowledge and understanding in human form. Even though he chooses us and calls us into righteousness we must still seek him with all our heart and say yes to him in return. In doing so, we will find the one who is wisdom itself, and all will be revealed.

If the world does not accept Jesus as Lord and Saviour, isn't this why it does not understand or embrace wisdom? Through his parables Jesus often took those held to be wise in the world and showed them to be foolish. Through the Beatitudes we know he takes the foolish things of this world and makes them wise. Both teachings reveal to us that only in God's kingdom the truth of wisdom can be seen. Didn't the great philosophers throughout the ages turn their backs on God? They thought they didn't need him, only to be proven wrong in their thinking as the years rolled by. 1 Corinthians 1:18-19 tells us the message of the cross is foolishness to those who are perishing, but to we who are saved, it is the power of God. Referencing Isaiah 29:14 Paul writes, 'For it is written: 'I will destroy the wisdom of the wise; the intelligence of the intelligent I will frustrate' (Corinthians 1:19). There are examples of God's work frustrating the accepted wisdom of the world throughout the Bible.

Let us look at the birth of Christ for instance. All the years of divination and all the sorcerers they had in Jerusalem, yet King Herod didn't know of Jesus' birth. Oh, how they were made to look foolish! The Bible says wise men came looking for they knew a very special child has been born (Matthew 2:1-12). This was the first the palace had heard of the news! The wise men, or Magi, came from a long way over hills and valleys, being led by a bright star in the night sky. Seeing how foolish King Herod was, they found Jesus and then left without returning to the palace as they had been asked to do. For they were working in God's wisdom, not their own, as the sorcerers of Herod were.

Where were the wise and the philosophers in the days of Christ, I wonder? Even as he grew up among the Pharisees, bright and righteous as they were, they couldn't work out where this very ordinary person came who was upsetting their everyday life, even after many years of living among them. When Jesus reached his thirtieth year and began to preach and teach amongst them, they began to take notice of him, yet he was still a puzzle to them (1 Corinthians 1:20).

I believe God turned the traditional ideas of wise people upside down to make people think for themselves and to shame the ones in power who had chosen the weak things of the world instead of leading their people in strength. He chose the lowly and despised such as women and Samaritans to shame the Jewish leaders into action. When God uses the poor and the feeble, no one may boast their works are in their own strength, but they will boast it is due to God's power working through them. We have this power because of who we are in Christ Jesus (2 Corinthians 5:17). Therefore, let him who boasts do so only in the Lord.

Take a look at the leaders of the world right now. Do we see this pattern working out in our here and now? Can we honestly say our leaders at the moment are wise? I don't think so. We shouldn't think we are cleverer than God, for he will easily catch us out in our arrogance. So let us remind ourselves not to get too big headed about living in Christ's ways since we are all human beings and all flesh and blood. But all can be ours if we follow Jesus and lean on his wisdom. Remember, Solomon believed wisdom is life. Jesus is my life. Is he yours?

Prayer

Thank you, Heavenly Father, for being the constant presence of wisdom in our lives. Thank you for being here, always. Help us now, Lord, to try and walk in humbleness as you did, not running ahead of you as young children who know no bounds but by your side as reverent disciples. Help us to develop the spirit of patience and wait on you, for what you say you will do I believe will happen. I want to be part of it, Lord. Teach us your ways, dear Jesus. Thank You, Lord.

Amen.

75

BE GENEROUS
(2 CORINTHIANS 8:1)

I t is very important as Christians to give generously, as our Lord and Father has given to us. This includes giving financially to support our church and serving as our pastors ask. However, our generosity should go beyond the church, and should not be only with our money. Even though money is very important, our generosity should extend to the giving of oneself, and one's time, if one is able to give in such a way.

Peter tells us that we are called to the royal priesthood (1 Peter 2:9), so we don't need to wait for the local priest or pastor to tell us what to do. We have God's permission and guidance through the Holy Spirit. Samuel told Saul when he was anointed that the Holy Spirit would come upon him and whatever his hand found to do he should do it, for God would be with him (1 Samuel 10:7). If we develop the love of God in our heart, we will just want to get involved, we won't be able to help ourselves. We have got the weak and frail in our midst and in the church, our spiritual fervour should be there for them. We have also got people shielding from COVID-19. We should reach out to the community in every way possible so that we are not only serving inside the church walls, even though the church should come first.

According to Paul's second letter to the Corinthians, out of the most severe trials overflowing joy can be found and out of extreme poverty wells up rich generosity (2 Corinthians 8:2). For he testifies that the early Christians gave as much as they were able, some even beyond their ability, which tells me that many sacrifices were made. They gave themselves first to the Lord and then to the leadership of the church, in keeping with God's will. We must remember that verse 9 of this chapter reminds us of the grace of our Lord Jesus Christ, who was rich yet became poor for us in every way. I must say, along with the teaching of Christ Jesus our Lord in the Beatitudes (see Chapter 40), we have no excuse for not knowing how to behave in our daily walk with the Lord.

Even if we go to church and attend Bible Study regularly, God can still say he does not know us when Judgement Day comes (see Matthew 25:31-46, The Parable of the Sheep and the Goats). When we think we are walking with the Lord, we need to think again if we are only doing it for those we love. Still, the Lord says the least we do is precious in his sight. He also tells us what we do for the weak, frail, sick, lame, prisoners, foreigners, neighbours or strangers; the least we do for them, we will be doing it for him. We must also remember in entertaining strangers, that we might be entertaining angels (Hebrews 13:2). So, we really do have to be careful how we live, how we intend to live and how we think of living for Christ Jesus every day.

When our Lord told the story of The Good Samaritan (Luke 10:25-37) to the crowds listening in Judea, he told them to go and do as the Samaritan had, generously looking after the victim left at the roadside in need. I'm not saying we need to go out and look for accident or assault victims to support. But I am saying we should make time for each other, thus making time for our Lord. We don't have to make a song and dance about it, as our Lord described in Matthew 6, but we ought to show each other love as God shows to us – Agape love. This type of love is that which demonstrates caring for one another. It can be seen wherever God has shown generosity, towards the just and the unjust alike. We are called to show the same love, with generosity as God's hands on this Earth.

Prayer

I will sing your praises, Lord, Oh I will sing your praises. I will continue to talk about you and worship you with thanksgiving in my heart and praise on my lips. I will delight myself in you, my Lord and King. As you have been generous to me, help me to give generously in return. You gave me all I have, and to you, I give it all back in service to others.

Bless your churches, O Lord our God. Where your people gather together to bring corporate worship to you, bless them Lord. Bless the ministers, pastors and leaders to whom you give the honour and privilege of welcoming your people. Please God, give them the wisdom to use the gifts they are given wisely in your name. Help them to lead us in helping others. For we want to be a Godly people, serving others as you served us Jesus. Thank you for all you have done for us.

Amen.

76

TRUE SATISFACTION

I have heard the story told of a man who stepped into a travel agency asking to go on a cruise. The attendant at the desk asked, 'Where do you want to go, sir?' 'I don't know' the man replied. The staff member suggested that the customer could look at the globe which sat in their office space. The man thought that was a good idea, so he started looking at the world in front of him. Such a long time he spent looking and spinning the globe until he got so frustrated and exclaimed, 'Is this all you have to offer?'

This poor man did not have a clue what he wanted or where he wanted to go. He literally had the whole world in his hands, and he could not decide where he wanted to go. It still was not enough for him. While reflecting on this story in the context of our church life, I saw a theme emerge. There are so many of us who seem to get everything but just seem to want more – even though we do not actually know what it is we want more of. Yet we already have everything we need right in front of us if we only look at it.

In Judges 9:1-6, one of Gideon's sons went to kill all of his 70 brothers after his father had died, to claim everything for himself. He succeeded, apart from the youngest who managed to hide. Although this son, Abimelech, was already rich and well provided for by his father, he wanted more. He wanted to take everything for himself. In the end, Abimelech called one of his own servants to kill him during an uprising, after a woman cracked open his skull with a millstone. He was too ashamed to be spoken of as the King killed by a woman. Evil men always get their just rewards from God. This is just one such biblical story of greed, and there are many, many more.

The world is full of things that can appeal to all of us, both good things and sinful things. Keeping ourselves apart from the sinful things, we can and should enjoy Christ Jesus in the fullness of his creation. For example, I go out for meals with friends, which can warm our hearts as we meet together as the fellowship of believers. We can and should be able to have a good laugh and enjoy the beauty and wonder of creation. If we are able to and so inclined, we should do things like going on cruises and taking time out, to consider and admire the changing of seasons and the glory of God's world. Let your imagination be stretched by the wonder of God's creations and stand in awe of God himself. Admire the glorious splendour of all he has made and worship him for all he has done.

If we actively pay attention to the world around us, that

should quench our thirst and satisfy our longings. Otherwise, we can agree with Solomon that all is vanity (Ecclesiastes 12:8). God warns us through his prophet Isaiah, in Chapter 55:1-3, about avoiding fruitless labour which cannot satisfy. The Rolling Stones, that great rock and roll group of the 1960s, had a great hit with the song 'I can't get no Satisfaction', even though they had all the money they could come by, all the food and drink and everything the world had to offer them, they still could not get satisfaction because they were not eating of the life-giving food of God. Only by living for God through Christ Jesus can we experience true satisfaction. As the songwriter, Stuart Townend declares, in Christ alone our hope is found.

Paul tells us to imitate Christ if we wish to gain true satisfaction (Philippians 2:1-18). It is not at all easy to imitate Christ Jesus but nobody said it would be easy. Is anything worth having ever easy? Jesus shows us how to live in the four Gospels telling the story of his life, and Paul tells us in this Bible passage to conduct ourselves in a manner that is worthy of the teachings we have received. If we do so, we should not go wrong.

My friends, it is so true. All we need is to be in Christ and to find his bread of life. In eating of him through communion, we will surely find true satisfaction. For remember, it is only through Christ we can reach the one true God himself and gain the abundant life we are promised as his children.

Prayer

Blessed Lord, we thank you that your prophet Isaiah has called us to heed his words, encouraging us to come to you for our true satisfaction. We praise you that we can come to you for our daily bread. That every day we can eat, drink and be satisfied through your generous providence. Help us to choose well as we discern which things in life appeal to us, and in doing so find the enjoyment and abundance of life that has been set out for us. May we always seek and find the Lord in the full knowledge that he will give us rest. Bless us all, dearest God.

Amen.

77

PEACE

Jesus says to us 'Peace I leave with you, my peace I give to you. I do not give to you as the world gives.' (John 14:27). I wonder if you truly know that peace which Jesus promises us. The peace which passes all understanding. Even in the midst of the wildest storms in life, we ought to have peace. Why? Because Jesus is the Prince of Peace. He gave us peace himself, and he is the embodiment of peace. If we are truly in him, and he in us, peace should always be part of our lives.

The path to finding peace is narrow since there isn't a lot of peace in the world around us. Too many things distract us from finding peace within us, the peace God wants us to have and has laid on our hearts for us. He promises us abundant life, and we can't have that without peace. There are a lot of peace stealers around. For example, being disobedient to God can steal your peace. If you are a godly person and you disobey God you will not find peace until you have repented, and the Holy Spirit has settled again within you. Even your own thoughts can steal your peace. If you spend too much of your time thinking about yourselves, your wants, desires or needs, eventually you will lose your peace because you have left Christ out of your thinking. Do this too often, and that is when anxiety and doubts can creep in. So, I say, even when it is hard, the narrow road to peace is so much better. For that is the path to eternal life.

Reflection

The famous prayer for peace is often attributed to St Francis' calls upon God to make us instruments of his peace. To be an instrument, or a tool, for peace in the life of another, we first need to find peace within ourselves. Ask God to help you be at peace with yourself today, so you can share your peace with your family, friends, community and church.

78

SEEK YE FIRST THE KINGDOM OF GOD (MATTHEW 6:33)

Matthew 6:33 tells us to seek first the kingdom of heaven and God's righteousness, then all things will fall into place. In this, God is reassuring us there is great reward in following his ways. I firmly believe this to be a fact. I wrote in Chapter 13 of this book that we can make bad decisions while we are in the middle of a storm. But if we walk with the Lord, he will be with us in the midst of whatever storms we face in life. Therefore, if he is with us, he can calm the storm. Have faith, for what he has done for one of his children he can do for all.

Let us take a quick look at some of the incredible things God has done for his children. In Daniel 3:19-27, King Nebuchadnezzar ordered Shadrach, Meshach and Abednego to be thrown into the fiery furnace. It was so hot the soldiers who threw them in died from getting too close! However, the three men did not die, and there appeared someone else whom we are told looked like the son of a god.

Nebuchadnezzar called the men back out of the furnace, and they didn't even get singed. Then there was Enoch. He walked with God faithfully all of his life, and we are told he didn't die physically. The Bible just says he was no more, God took him away (Genesis 5:24). Enoch was granted an eternity of walking physically with God due to his devotion to him.

At that time of Enoch, Genesis 4:26 tells us man began to call upon the Lord with their concerns. As I wrote in Chapter 20, this is what is missing in our society today. Men are not calling on God or seeking him as we ought to, in spite of everything we know about his providence and goodness. The world has come a long way since Genesis was written and of course, knowledge has increased vastly, yet instead, we go forward mentally but backwards spiritually. The two parts of our lives are not joined. Mortal man behaves as if we are indestructible, but the last few years have shown we are absolutely not.

We can sometimes repair each part of our lives or our bodies that are broken, but not always and certainly not on our own. We need God. Anyone who says we do not is fooling themselves. Men often think we know better but we do not. We know we did not make ourselves, we had to come from somewhere! Deny it if you wish but as Christians, we know that there is a power beyond all power, and we need him in our lives. We know there is a God, all powerful and everlasting, above all Gods. I know we'd rather not talk about him, but the world could not exist without him – and the world includes us. Whatever we make of him, God is the ruler of the world and mortal man is nothing without him. That's the plain truth of it.

Genesis 6:8 tells us Noah found favour in the eyes of God. The God of the universe with infinite power who created all things took an interest in one man from Mesopotamia. How fantastic is that? But how about us? Can the Lord say that of us these days? Would he find favour in us if he focused on our lives? This is an accolade reserved for a select number in the Bible. There are two people mentioned in Deuteronomy 1, apart from Moses who is delivering the message from God. They are Caleb and Joshua, who are appointed leaders amongst the Israelites. The Bible says they walked wholeheartedly with the Lord and have entered the promised land. They entered God's rest and the fulfilment of the Lord came through in their lives because they obeyed the Lord at every step. They trusted God, believed in him and in his Word, honoured him, respected him, and their lives went well because of it. They remembered where they were coming from, where they were headed and who was leading them there with a mighty and outstretched hand. They are true models of how to live with God so everything will fall into place. Moses was their natural leader, but God was their supernatural leader, guide and shepherd.

The Lord was with Jehoshaphat because he rejected the gods of the world and was devoted to God (2 Chronicles

17:3-6). As his father, David, had been before him. We all make mistakes from time to time, as David surely did, but there is always a way back to the Lord our God. His providence is endless, recounted throughout the ages in the Bible. He even provided the ultimate way out of our mistakes by sending His precious Son Jesus Christ to die and cover our sins. I have already said he is a God of second chances (see Chapter 68). So, we do not have to fight and struggle to make amends. We just have to repent and continue our walk with him. Seek him, and we will find the kingdom of God every day of our lives through his providence and love.

Reflection

I started off this chapter with the verse from Matthew 6, 'Seek ye first the kingdom of God and His righteousness'. That really is the only way to live. When we want to make a decision, when we want to find a way forward or when we want to acknowledge our mistakes, we should always humble ourselves and go to God. We should seek his face like David did (Psalm 27:8). For our God is merciful and compassionate. He is willing and longing to hold us in his arms, as a hen gathers her chicks. The God of David, Moses, Caleb and Joshua is the very same God of today. He is, was and always will be. Let us, as his children, take hold of Jesus' teachings and put them into action today.

79

THE GOD OF YESTERDAY
(HEBREWS 13:8)

The God of yesterday is still the God of today and he will be the God of tomorrow too. He has got the surest telephone number and he is always at home so the landline will always be answered (see Chapter 25). This is one of the promises he made to us as his children. Whatever situation we are in, wherever we are, if we call upon God, he will answer us with his providence. Is that not wonderful?

We have got such a great wall of strength and power to call upon in our Lord Jesus Christ. That is amazing! Our God promised when we returned to him in repentance and humbleness that he would heal our wounds and forgive our iniquities. This leads me to ask why God is even bothering with us, when we all know that God could use anyone he wants – even an animal – to do his bidding? Remember the donkey that God used to correct Balaam's actions in Numbers 22:21-35?

I believe God wants his name to be renowned in all the world, as is declared in Jeremiah 33:9, therefore he uses as many of us as possible to make that happen. However, this is difficult to recognise if we look at the state of the world right now. COVID-19 has truly swept the globe, with 6.5 million deaths (and rising) across every single country and no sign of when things are going to end. I have wept so many times since the pandemic started. There has been many a day when I could not stop my tears from falling. Yet we all know God is waiting for the world to come to him in prayer and penitence, then he will act.

In 2 Chronicles 7:14, God says if my people would only humble themselves and come to Him in prayer, he would heal our land – and how our land needs healing. Our government does not know what to do. Doctors and scientists keep trying but nobody knows what to do. Yet I have not heard of any churches, leaders or plans from such organisations to get together and call upon the Lord. God is waiting for his people to return to him in humble adoration. He would answer our prayer, he has said so. He is the God of yesterday, he never goes back on his words. What he says he will do, he will do. So let us take up our responsibility to intercede for the world and worry him with our prayers.

Prayer

Lord, I wonder if you still think there is no one to stand in the gap and intercede for your world. Those of us who know you as our God and Father continue to pray for your people. You hear our cries, even if there are only a few of us left to speak them. I remember Elijah telling you that he was the only one left in his time, when you, O God, let him know that you have reserved thousands of people who will not bow their knees to idols. So, Lord, I do not believe I am the only one that feels this way about the plague of COVID-19. I know you have people praying to you and I rejoice in this.

I pray, Lord, that you will join my prayer with all the others from all peoples across all nations in the world. I ask for your forgiveness for whatever has displeased you, causing this plague upon the world. I humbly ask for your forgiveness and grace. We are all undeserving people, yet I am asking in the knowledge you tell us to come to you in faith. You are our God and our Father; to whom shall I go if not to you? There is none like you. So I am asking you in the name of Jesus, our Lord and Saviour, to intervene in the pandemic today. Thank you for hearing my prayer and for what you are going to do in our world.

Amen.

80

RENEW OUR WORSHIP VOW

I n Chapter 79, I explored the Bible passage 2 Chronicles 7:14 which tells us God waits for us to reach out to him in faith, and he promises to respond. Jeremiah 33:3 underlines God's promise, that if we call out to him, he will answer. How often do we take him up on this offer though?

Sometimes we may feel like we have failed Jesus and therefore cannot turn to him. Jesus told us to act wisely, but we do not always manage to. We have to be careful and guard our hearts, so our motivations remain true. Likewise, we have to be wise, and we do not always manage. Many times, we get hurt, sometimes badly, yet we must open up ourselves up to continued love and grace as God calls us to do. We must make ourselves available for God to use us – for that is true worship.

If we give all things to God and take our concerns to him in prayer, he will give us the strength to continue and worship him through our actions. We can surrender all in his name. Paul encourages us with these words from Galatians 5:10,

'The one who is throwing you into confusion, whoever that may be, will have to pay the penalty.' Our confusion is not our burden to bear, it is the enemies, and Jesus is ready to help us work everything out. However many times we come back to him and renew our worship vow, he will be there to listen, respond and give us his fatherly love.

Prayer

Oh, Lord, how much do we need your healing hands upon our land? We know we do, but only you alone know how much, Lord. We need you, God, to heal our church, school, government, family, community, friends and our land far and wide where there is so much disturbance. May our prayers of sadness turn to prayers of gladness as we cry out in worship today, asking you to renew us once again, so we can be part of the solution in your world.

Amen.

81

A PRAYER FOR ALL

Our God and Father of our Lord Jesus Christ, if it pleases you to hear this prayer at this particular time, I beseech you to listen. My prayer to you, O God, is to ask you to draw us closer to you through your mighty power and infinite grace. May these few minutes we spend with you in prayer be full of the true spirit of supplication. Grow in us a daily habit, a desire to spend more and more time with you in prayer.

Lord of all our days. Grant that none of us with closed eyes may spend our days looking into the mirror of vanity. May our eyes be turned away from everything but the spiritual and divine. May we have communion with you now, O Lord, in the secret place of your sanctuary. Holy Father, you know how hard it is for us to rid our minds of the distractions and thoughts around us, but I pray now, dearest Lord, that you will help us to focus. Give us the strength, through prayer, to draw the sword of faith against every kind of distraction and fight, as Abraham did when he drove away the birds which swooped down to spoil his offering of sacrifice to you. Help us now as we pray to cast off fear, doubt and anxiety, so that we can enjoy that sweet fellowship with you, Father, Son and Holy Spirit.

We adore you, dearest Father and eternal King. We worship the Holy Trinity, God who was and is and is to come. Holy and most righteous God, we worship you this day and always. May all the churches across all the nations worship you this day. Renew your will in us, that we may go out as you have commanded us, to go and tell the good news of your kingdom throughout the world. Help us to put on the full armour of faith and carry the knowledge of your holy presence with us always. Empower us as we speak of the Kingdom of God and spread the Good News of Jesus Christ the Messiah, thus making your name even more renowned.

May our whole selves overflow with your holy presence, today and always. May we always be quick to say, 'Here I am, send me.' Thank you, Heavenly Father, for hearing me today at this particular time. I submit my prayer to you in the name of he who is above all names, Lord Jesus Christ.

Amen.

Appendices

APPENDIX 1

WORDS OF ENCOURAGEMENT: GOD'S PROMISES CONTINUE (ISAIAH 41: 8-13)

These are some of the Lord's promises towards us, his children, those whom he has taken out of Egypt. Those whom he has taken out of the iron smelting furnace. Those whom he takes from the wilderness experiences. Those whom the Lord removed the navel cords from our naked bodies and cleansed from us our guilt and shame. These words are from God, the great I AM.

He says:

But you Israel, my servant' [meaning Jacob, or Pearl, or you] 'whom I have chosen, you descendants of Abraham my friend,

I took you from the ends of the earth, from its farthest corners I called you.

I said, "You are my servant"; I have chosen you and have not rejected you.

So do not fear, for I am with you; do not be dismayed, for I am your God.

I will strengthen you and help you; I will uphold you with my
righteous right hand.
All who rage against you will surely be ashamed and disgraced;
those who oppose you will be as nothing and perish.
Though you search for your enemies, you will not find them.
Those who wage war against you will be as nothing at all.
For I am the Lord your God who takes hold of your right hand
and says to you, do not fear; I will help you.

Now all I can say is this. Glorious things are spoken about
you, our God. I join whoever says these glorious and
wonderful things of you by saying glorious things have been
spoken about you. Thank you, O God, for the words of the
Bible.

Prayer

Open for me, O God, the gates of righteousness, that
I may go in and join your inheritance in bringing
righteous offerings to you. For you have become my
salvation. You are the stone the builder has rejected.
Now you are my capstone. Thank you, oh my God.
Amen.

APPENDIX 2

IMPORTANT WORDS & PASSAGES OF SCRIPTURE

would like to share some words and passages from scripture that matter very much to me. May they prove to be useful, even meaningful, to you, the reader of this book.

1. Isaiah 43 has been an anchor for me in recent years. As I continue to read it and grow familiar with it, it gets better and better for me spiritually. Verses one to seven and it goes on right on to the end.

2. Isaiah 46:4 was very important to me at a time when I really needed to hear from God. It was Good Friday, my son was very ill in the hospital and my husband and I were under a lot of pressure. This verse brought me great comfort in that situation.

3. John 17:3-6. In early April 2017, this chapter become so very special to me. It opened up the windows of my mind and my heart, to let me see and understand

how much I am in Christ and he is in me. The whole of my faith became very true to me. Most of all, I knew God prayed for me at that time. Thank you, Lord Jesus.

4. Romans 5:5-6: 'And hope does not put us to shame, because God's love has been poured out into our hearts through the Holy Spirit, who has been given to us. You see, at just the right time, when we were still powerless, Christ died for the ungodly.'

5. Romans 8:11: 'And if the Spirit of him who raised Jesus from the dead is living in you, he who raised Christ from the dead will also give life to your mortal bodies because of his Spirit who lives in you.' Praise the Lord!

6. Romans 12:2 is an incredibly important verse for me in my Christian life. I always want to praise God who is constantly working out his purposes for his children. He guides me and holds me together throughout good times and bad. Thanks be to God for his great wisdom.

7. 2 Corinthians 6:1-2. This one surprises me. When I read it, it is as if God has spoken to me directly. I take it on as a solemn promise.

8. Another Bible passage that surprises me every time I return to it is the whole Book of 1 Thessalonians. Pastor Bruce Stoke once preached a series of sermons on 1 Thessalonians and after he did this, I could not stop reading it. The message of the letter seemed to go into my body and course through my veins. It speaks so closely to me and encourages me a great deal. Through this book the Holy Spirit has spoken to me many times; for example, I was once reading chapter 4 of 1 Thessalonians, and the Holy Spirit directed my attention to Hebrews 1:1-2 where I received further blessing.

9. We know that our Lord Jesus Christ is God with us from the Old Testament times. He is the Alpha and the Omega, the beginning and the end, the Son of God and that's a fact. This message is given to us very clearly in the Book of Revelation, and I value this verse very much (Revelation 22:13).

APPENDIX 3

LUKE'S WRITING TO THEOPHILUS: EXPLORING THE AUTHORSHIP OF LUKE AND ACTS

Sometime during the last year of Jesus' ministry here on Earth, while he was walking around Judea and teaching his disciples, Jesus began to tell them that he was going to be killed. Luke records many of these instances in his writings to his friend Theopolis, which we now know as the Gospel of Luke and the Book of Acts. Luke was not one of Jesus' disciples, maybe because he was a doctor, but he was part of the large movement that followed the news about Jesus as it spread. Some believe it was Peter who instructed Luke to collect these stories of Jesus' life and early Christianity, so he had access to first-hand accounts from the people he wrote about and was well informed.

Luke began his work by writing a letter to a friend of the name Theophilus, who himself didn't follow Jesus, but really wanted to know about him. In both the Gospel of Luke and the Book of Acts, Luke addresses Theophilus by name in the opening verses. This gives us confidence the two books are written by the same person, a series of texts exploring what came during the life of Jesus, and what came after. Some people believe the Book of Acts is an unfinished book, but Luke himself writes he has investigated all things from beginning to end so he can give a full account of matters (Luke 1:3). Therefore, I am sure he has written all there is to share, and as the Gospel of John states, no one could write down all that he did, as no book could hold it (John 21:25).

I personally love the Gospel of Luke. It is my favourite of all the gospels. Luke tells us Jesus began his ministry well, but he did not get a lot of time since he was killed at a young age. He lived only 33 and a half years, yet he would teach all his teachings and do all he came to Earth to do in only three and a half years (see Chapter 60). What he did during this time changed the whole world. Luke says many things about Jesus which we use in our worship songs today, so great are his words.

Luke told Theophilus that Jesus was the stone the builder rejected yet he became the cornerstone (see Chapter 68). He never did any wrong, yet he was rejected as the builders reject impure stone. His enemies thought they had killed Jesus, that he was finished, but now he is more alive than ever before. Luke wrote to tell Theophilus about the resurrection, the Road to Emmaus, the dreadful betrayal at the Last Supper and many miracles of Jesus in his ministry. He was never wrong, nor did he leave anyone in a worse position than he met them. He healed the sick or those with blinded eyes, cleansed the lepers, straightened crooked bones, drove out demons, calmed the storm and he even raised Lazarus giving him back to their family alive and well.

Luke continued the story of Jesus in Acts 1 as he was taken back to heaven. He told his disciples to wait in Jerusalem as his father would send something special for them – and us. We are promised power from on high in the form of the Holy Spirit, enabling us to continue the work Jesus started (Acts 1:8). In the Gospel of John, the writer testifies that Jesus promised when they received the Holy Spirit, they would do even greater work than he himself was doing (John 14:12-14). So the story about Jesus will continue to be told throughout the world.

So it is, even though Jesus Christ called out from the cross that 'It is finished' his teaching has not finished at all. His healing, his inspiration, all that he has done is not finished. What has finished is his mission on Earth. He came to pay the debt that we could not pay, the debt of our sin. He pays it all for everyone in the whole world, past, present and future. Jesus had a short life on Earth, but his finished work will last forever.

When Jesus said from the cross 'It is finished' he meant the price is paid for everyone. So, the world must know how it was paid. Luke and his friends knew this, and through his books, Luke passes on his knowledge to us, so we who accept Luke's writings as truth can in turn pass the story on. It is the story of deliverance, freedom and liberty. Luke tells us about Jesus, so we have the choice to believe in his ways and follow our destinies with him. The story of Jesus is the greatest story ever told, and yet it is all fact.

APPENDIX 4

A PRAYER DURING COVID-19

Almighty God, the most righteous and eternal Lord who is awesome in judgement and upright in truth. I, your child, do venture to approach the foot of your throne. I come in the name of your glorious son Jesus Christ, thanking you for the privilege given to one like me to do so. I acknowledge the privilege and honour you bestow upon me in allowing me to approach your throne as you do. Thank you, Father.

Thank you also, Heavenly Father, for allowing me to intercede on behalf of others. Your mercy is beyond measure in this wonderful opportunity you have bestowed upon me. I remember, O Lord, you spoke to one of your prophets, Isaiah, telling him that you look for someone to stand in the gap. You seek those brave enough to intercede for your people, but often have been unable to find them. Holy Father, here I am doing so now. Be pleased to accept my plea.

I know you are already aware of what I am about to say to you in this, my prayer, but we must come to you in humble adoration and ask of you whatever is on our hearts anyway. We are your children, and to come to you as the little children do is blessed. So I come, Holy Father. I bring my prayer to you.

As we face the continued COVID-19 pandemic, I thank you for the vaccines you have sent to help us. The world cried out to you in prayer, and you provided people with the knowledge to develop the science we needed. Father, I thank you so much for your providence. What more can I say? It is a modern-day miracle. Words are not enough to express my thanks, Lord, but they are all I have for now. Please accept our thanks and praise which you fully deserve; I will go on thanking you and praising you with every breath you have given me for the rest of my days.

I pray for all the encouragers who are working tirelessly, doing their best and guiding others through this very difficult time, as we see so many ill, so many deaths around us and so many shielding in their homes. O Lord, I see so much anxiety in the world. Rates of loneliness, mental illness and domestic abuse are rising. I ask Lord, in your mercy, to hear our prayer. Have mercy upon us and come to our aid.

I know we are a wicked and adulterous generation, turning to our idols and then returning to seek help from you. Even when you have warned us over and over about our behaviour, we are so stiff necked and rebellious against you. I recognise we deserve nothing from you, Lord, as I acknowledge our disobedience to you. Yet God, to whom shall we go if not you? We are your children, whomever we are. We are your creation and you love us.

Please, Lord, come and remove this virus from the world. Rid us of this burden which is causing so much hurt and sadness in the heart. Please, Holy Father, forgive our foolish and wicked ways, whatever they may be. Guide us back to your path and focus our eyes on you. Strengthen our spirits and give us boldness of character to speak your truth where it is needed. That we may in turn guide our brothers and sisters to the light of your love and hope.

Father God, if it may please you to increase my faith and the gifts you've given me to serve you with, then let it be so. Increase the spirit of discernment in me I pray, that I may hear from you more often and worship you more dearly. I ask all these things in the name of your glorious son Jesus Christ.

Amen.

ABOUT THE AUTHOR

Pearl Lennon was born in Jamaica and came to the UK in the 1960s. She worked in healthcare and in caring roles, whilst honing her craft as a seamstress and, together with her husband Justice, raising a family of six children and looking after a great many more. Pearl became a Christian in the 1990s, serving as a Deacon in Woodgrange Baptist Church for almost 20 years. Always creative, Pearl's faith and artistic inclinations meet in this book.

StoryTerrace